W9-BCD-008

Why Johnny Should Learn Foreign Languages

Why Johnny Should Learn Foreign Languages

Theodore Huebener

Director of Foreign Languages in the Schools of New York City

CHILTON COMPANY · BOOK DIVISION

Publishers

PHILADELPHIA AND NEW YORK

Published in Philadelphia by Chilton Company,
and simultaneously in Toronto, Canada, by Ambassador Books, Ltd.

LIBRARY OF CONGRESS CATALOG CARD NUMBER 61-5362

DESIGNED BY WILLIAM E. LICKFIELD
MANUFACTURED IN THE UNITED STATES OF AMERICA
BY QUINN & BODEN COMPANY, INC., RAHWAY, N. J.

Foreword

THIS excellent little book, by a distinguished educator to whom the teachers' profession, parents, former schoolboys, and the American public at large owe a huge debt of gratitude, could hardly be more timely. After years of apparent indifference, the challenge of the Sputnik, the stern criticism of many high-minded guides of public opinion (such as Walter Lippmann, John Maynard Hutchins, James Conant), and the sad realization of our failure to make this country rightly understood abroad, have aroused us to the need to improve our educational system and in particular to strengthen the study of modern languages and mathematics in American schools and colleges. The case for more, better, and more effective teaching of languages is put here concisely and cogently. An impressive array of arguments is marshalled, all resting on factual data and on precise figures. No appeal to sentiment is made unduly; no cultural superiority is claimed for either the humanists or the so-called leisure classes who have enjoyed opportunities to study a foreign tongue or to travel abroad. Languages today are useful for all or nearly all, in direct or indirect fashion. They are indispensable for a growing number of Americans, in a country where 50 per cent of high school boys and girls go to college. There is no propaganda for any cause in stating the truths formulated and strongly supported here, except in the original and legitimate sense of the word in which propaganda means the propagation of a reasoned faith. Dr. Huebener's fervent loyalty goes first, not to his profession, not to any one subject, but to his country and to those who have the future of America at heart.

We need not develop an inferiority complex and childishly overpraise the Russians or other European nations which order these things differently, and perhaps better. American education mirrors American history, answers American conditions, and voices the goals and ideals of American society. But in it are certain lags and some routine and apathy. For several decades, it seemed possible to consider that the United States had reached a high level of prosperity and a plateau on which the country could complacently remain unconcerned with the rest of the world. The implicit goal of education was to train youth to fit into that almost static society, to "get along" with people, to eschew foreign entanglements, to banish tragedy, and to enjoy a progress often conceived as primarily technological. Between 1920 and 1940, foreign languages sank to a low estate in our curricula; the study of other living cultures suffered neglect just as the world was shrinking around us and as any move attempted five thousand miles away could involve us, willy-nilly, in broils which might turn into wars. We preached isolation at the very time when it became impossible to practice it. We pretended that we could remain untouched by the woeful fate of peoples of other continents, thus forgetful of the profound sense of commitment in Americans and of the ideal of fraternity which had always, as it does today, prompted us to proclaim in the words of John Keats that "the miseries of the world are misery, and will not let us rest."

Things have changed, but they are still far from satisfactory. Dr. Huebener clearly demonstrates that, in almost every great country, the proportion of pupils and students mastering one or two languages is considerably greater than in the United States. Yet no country today is more universally involved in world problems. The task of leading the free world has devolved upon us, and we cannot shirk it. Into Europe, into South America, into the Congo, Morocco, Nigeria, into Saudi Arabia, Iran, Laos, and Vietnam, thousands of Americans are sent every year, in diplomacy, trade, banking, in the administration of economic assistance or of technical aid, in hygiene, in the aviation and oil industries—people who are not competent to fulfill their assigned roles if they are language blind. The Hoover Commission has proclaimed it; Dr. Conant has repeated it; new directives require foreign languages for entering the Foreign Service (which was unbelievably short-sighted, some years ago, to drop that requirement). The knowledge of at least one tongue other than one's own yields profits, tangible and, even more precious, intangible.

Dr. Huebener has stressed the tangible advantages of such a study; they should indeed be rated high in a country which believes itself to be practically minded, but which in truth is also idealistic and religious and is, under our very eyes, achieving a momentous scientific and cultural revolution. We have hurt ourselves economically through our willful neglect of languages; we have deprived our children of opportunities which lay within their reach; we have allowed them to believe that a study which they imagine to be difficult could, or should, frighten them—a very un-American creed.

But we have hurt our national interest and our foreign policy even more by that neglect, and jeopardized the unique world position which was ours at the end of World War II, when America was the cynosure and the Mecca of all the war-ridden but hopeful countries. The study of languages, besides its practical usefulness, is one of the most broadening we can undertake. It enables us to realize that other peoples feel, think, act differently from us and are justified in doing so, just as they are in treating their language, the mirror and the vehicle of their culture, reverently. The great scientist Thomas Huxley rightly stated once, in 1882, that most of the disagreements and misunderstandings arise out of mistakes and confusion over words. "One of the safest ways," he added, "of delivering yourself from the bondage of words is to know how ideas look in words to which you are not accustomed. That is one reason for the study of language . . . Another is that, from the learning of additional languages, you will know your own language better than ever you did."

Familiarity with one other language at least, acquired early, is the surest means for us to realize that the words which we bandy about most freely, such as "democracy," "capitalism," "colonialism," "imperialism," "free enterprise," and "free press," carry with them very different connotations even in languages similar to our own. Once we have gained such an awareness, we are ready to understand other nations and to speak to them within their "frame of reference." America has, in the last twenty years—and for the first time in history—asserted that the wealth of a prosperous nation is a sacred trust and should be used in part to assist underdeveloped countries. Yet she has reaped ingratitude, misunderstanding, ill will, and at times active hostility in many a corner.

One of the reasons for such a sad state of affairs is the inability of many Americans who went abroad and of many who stayed at home to enter into the moods of foreigners. We antagonized many by forcing our own language upon them and refusing to say ten words in their own. We thus failed to understand their psychology and we were accused of practicing economic and cultural imperialism. We have been misjudged, often unfairly.

But what is the use of blaming nations less fortunate than ours, writhing in the grip of difficult crises of growth? Our manifest destiny in the world in the present century is to be generous and patient, but also intelligent, and to look to the future constructively. To succeed—and history may not offer us a second chance if we fail—to unravel the tangled web of economic, military, political, psychological forces at work in the world, we need all the broadening of our minds, all the flexing of our intellectual muscles that we can muster. We have to be intelligent and informed as well as determined. And languages, as Dr. Huebener well shows, help us train our minds and answer the famous cry of an English poet in the Victorian age: "More brain, O Lord, more brain!"

HENRI PEYRE
Chairman, Dept. of Romance Languages
Yale University

Preface

SHOULD American youth be equipped with competence in foreign languages?

The answer seems so obvious, particularly at this time, that one would expect unqualified and enthusiastic approval from our leaders. Until very recently, however, this has not been the case. In fact, despite widespread popular interest in foreign languages, many educational administrators throughout the years have minimized their importance as a subject in our curriculum. That is why almost half the nation's high schools have offered no courses in this area and why it has been an elective, occupying a minor place in American education. Until a very recent reversal in policy, the trend among colleges was to lower the foreign language requirement for admission and not to require it for higher degrees.

Finally, even leaders in the field of foreign languages became discouraged. After a nation-wide survey, a committee of linguists accepted the situation and decided that the best they could hope to achieve in language courses was a modest competence in reading. And so the reading aim was adopted. Methods and procedures, textbooks and materials were improved but the basic attitude remained, namely, that foreign language study is a comparatively unimportant part of the American youngster's education.

Suddenly, because of the international position of the United States and rivalry with the Soviet Union, the situation has changed. Realizing the importance of knowledge of foreign languages in dealing with other peoples, the State Department is sponsoring elaborate programs for the training of its personnel. The voices of prominent citizens resound through the land, demanding a stronger language course in high school and college. Educational administrators are getting busy organizing courses in Russian. The trend in the colleges now is to increase foreign language requirements.

These are encouraging signs. They are, however, all outward manifestations of an eagerness to deal quickly with a glaring weakness. What is really needed is a fundamental change in attitude. Is the knowledge of a foreign language merely a cultural adornment, a useful tool, a helpful discipline, or is it one of the important factors in the educational equipment of every normal American child?

Our educators have prided themselves upon the fact that they have provided for the development of every aspect of the child's personality. Among the trite expressions used to stress this thought are: "Ours is a child-centered school," "We teach children, not subjects," and "We teach the whole child."

The basic aim is to develop the potentialities of the individual so that he will fit into his community. In their eagerness to educate the child for his environment, the educators have lost sight of the meaning of "community." They fail to realize that through modern means of communication and transportation the immediate environment has expanded to a much vaster community. It now extends to the furthest reaches of the globe—and beyond.

Yes, let us educate the *whole child,* but let us educate him for his *whole environment,* for the *whole community.* This includes the nation, the continent, the world. All our major relations—political, military, commercial, cultural—are worldwide. Now, any relation between groups of human beings is based on the exchange of ideas. The sole means of exchange is language. Through this medium alone can we find out what is in the minds of other peoples and what are their aspirations, their ambitions, their ideals.

Our present-day world does not, like the ancient world, consist of independent, self-sufficient nations. Due to the amazing increase in scientific knowledge, in inventions, and the multiplicity of raw materials used in the manufacture of many products, all nations have become dependent upon one another. The world has become one vast community which depends for its very existence on the sharing of ideas and the exchange of goods. Again, this exchange cannot be carried on efficiently without the use of language.

To compete successfully in foreign trade, we must be able to speak the languages of our customers. To progress in science, we must know what has been accomplished in laboratories in other countries, especially in the Soviet Union. It is silly to say that we can rely on interpreters. The research scientist who expects to do things and do them quickly, must be able to read abstracts in the foreign language. For travel that is to be really enjoyable, rewarding, and enriching, a knowledge of foreign languages is indispensable. And, most important of all, success in conducting our international relations is dependent upon language. The fact that we have been so amateurish in this sphere and have so frequently fumbled, is due in great part to the woeful incompetence of our foreign representatives in foreign languages.

At present a knowledge of foreign languages is not merely a desirable asset for Americans stationed abroad; it is absolutely imperative. Not only our progress and prosperity, our very survival depends on the character of our international relations.

We are spending vast sums to train scientists to produce terrifying machines of destruction. But so are the Soviets. Annihilation can be avoided only by discussion, by negotiation, by co-operation. As Governor Robert Meyner of New Jersey has said: "There is one and only one defense against a nuclear war—and that is peace."

Granted that conferences should replace conflicts, that language is the medium of international understanding: would it not suffice to train a sufficient number of linguists and diplomats to maintain contact with other nations? Why should the average high school student be compelled to learn a foreign language?

The answer is that we cannot wait until the student has become an adult. The best time, psychologically and educationally, to learn a language is during childhood and youth. It takes years of practice to master a language and to acquire oral fluency. The start must be made at an early age if a firm foundation is to be laid.

Furthermore, there must be a large reservoir of trained youth to draw upon. In a democracy, education must provide the widest possible opportunities for all. No one can predict with certainty the life career of any given pupil. Who knows whether the future ambassador to France may not be seated in Miss Jones' French class?

The acquisition of a foreign language will in no case be a loss; it will always be an asset. In addition to linguists—who will have to be given special training later anyway—our schools have the duty of equipping all normal pupils with the knowledge and skills necessary for an intelligent solution of world problems. First and foremost—not last—among these skills is competence in a foreign language. Furthermore, such competence is a definite economic asset. There are numerous interesting and lucrative jobs in business, in industry, in world trade, and in government for those who qualify.

In short, knowledge of a foreign language is not a cultural luxury; it is a practical necessity. It is needed in business, in travel, in research, and in the Foreign Service. It is needed for cultural exchange, for international understanding, for peace.

That is why Johnny should learn a foreign language!

Contents

Foreword by Henri Peyre . . . v
PREFACE . . . ix
1. POLYGLOT AMERICA . . . 1
2. THE U.S. IS CAUGHT SHORT . . . 10
Languages for Leisure—If at All . . . 10
A Rude Awakening . . . 15
3. WE ARE AT THE BOTTOM . . . 23
Foreign Languages—Strongest Subject in Foreign Schools . 23
Foreign Languages—Weakest Subject in American Schools . 36
4. WORLD LANGUAGES FOR WORLD CONTACTS . . . 42
A Tongue-Tied Leader . . . 42
World Trade Demands World Languages . . . 43
Foreign Languages—*Sine Qua Non* of the Foreign Service . 51
Foreign Missionaries Need Foreign Languages . . . 58
You Can Get By—But That's All! . . . 62
5. "But, Does It Pay to Know a Foreign Language?" . . . 64
Foreign Language Teachers Are Needed . . . 78
6. THE BABEL OF TONGUES . . . 80
In Western Europe . . . 80
In Eastern Europe . . . 95
In Africa . . . 100
In Asia . . . 103
Home Again . . . 109
Why Not One Language for the Whole World? . . . 115
7. WHERE DO WE GO FROM HERE? . . . 119
BIBLIOGRAPHY . . . 129
INDEX . . . 131

1 · *Polyglot America*

THE United States is usually referred to as one of the English-speaking, Anglo-Saxon nations. This is not quite accurate since scores of languages are spoken in America and since a great proportion of the American people is definitely not of Anglo-Saxon origin.

English, it is true, was the dominant language of the Colonies. The vast numbers of immigrants from abroad who came later adopted it, as they did the English common law and English social ideals. The use of a common language was a blessing. It made for political unity and gave the country cultural cohesion during two world wars.

This does not, however, minimize the fact that more than 42,000,000 persons of different languages and cultures came to our shores in little over a century. This huge migration of peoples is an epic in history. It is this vast influx of foreigners that transformed a group of struggling colonies with four million inhabitants into a powerful and wealthy nation of 175 millions within a century and a half.

According to the 1950 census, a total of 10,161,168 white persons were of foreign birth. The countries which had sent more than 200,000 each were:

Austria	408,785
Canada—French	238,409
Canada—other	756,153
Czechoslovakia	278,268

England and Wales	584,615
Germany	984,331
Hungary	268,022
Ireland	504,961
Italy	1,427,145
Mexico	450,562
Norway	202,294
Poland	861,184
Scotland	244,200
Sweden	324,944
U.S.S.R.	894,844

It is evident that the most numerous ethnic groups were the Italians, Germans, Russians, and Poles, in that order. Among the latter two were many Jews. None of these is Anglo-Saxon. Strictly speaking, a large proportion of those of British origin are not Anglo-Saxon, for the Scotch and Welsh, as well as the Irish are of Celtic blood.

This situation prevailed in America from the earliest days. New Amsterdam and the Hudson Valley were settled by the Dutch. Delaware was held by the Swedes. At the beginning of the eighteenth century there were so many Germans in Pennsylvania that it was considered a bilingual state. The French and the Spaniards had extensive settlements in the South. None of these groups was either Anglo-Saxon or English-speaking.

Let us look more closely at the major ethnic stocks that settled in our country.

Although America was settled predominantly by English-speaking peoples, i.e., English, Scotch, Welsh, and Irish, there was, right from the beginning, a steady influx of other ethnic groups. In fact, the latter had representatives here long before the famous settling of Plymouth by the Pilgrims in 1620. At Port Royal, in South Carolina, settled in 1562 by a company of Huguenots under Jean Ribault, there were Alsatian and Hessian Protestants. The earliest English settlement in America was Jamestown, founded in 1620, by the swashbuckling

Captain John Smith. In his *True Travels* he mentions Poles, Swiss, and Dutchmen, occasionally applying the epithet "damned" to the latter. Judging by the names given, some of the Dutchmen were really Germans.

French Huguenots came to Florida in 1564. The next year French settled Charleston, S.C. As far north as Maine and as far south as Louisiana, French traders and missionaries carried on their activities. They taught their language to the Indians and introduced their customs and their architecture. Although these influences have largely vanished, they are still evident in Louisiana.

In the Colonies the more affluent English-speaking residents esteemed French for its cultural value and hired French tutors to teach the language to their children. French continued to be popular and has maintained its prestige right up to the present time, although the number of immigrants from France has been rather small compared with other European stocks. Spaniards arrived in Florida one year after the French; they also settled in Louisiana. Through the cession of Florida in 1819 and through the Louisiana Purchase in 1803, large numbers of Spanish-speaking people became American citizens. Many more were added to the United States through the acquisition of California, New Mexico, and Texas after the Mexican War. They did not, however, exert any marked cultural influence on the English-speaking population.

In fact, Spanish, as a school subject, did not play any role until the Spanish-American War in 1898. Since then, and particularly from 1918 on, Spanish has established itself as one of the major foreign languages studied throughout the country. In many of the larger cities, like New York, it leads in enrollments.

The two foreign languages which have depended to a great extent, as school subjects, on the large number of people who speak them in this country, are German and Italian.

As mentioned above, Germans were present in the earliest settlements. The first substantial immigration, however, was that of 1683 when the gallant ship *Concord* brought a large company of Dissenters from the Rhine to Philadelphia at the invitation of William Penn. They founded Germantown, and were followed by considerable numbers of their compatriots who spread out in the South, the West, and New York. They started glassworks, paper mills, and printing presses. The first edition of the Bible printed in any European language in the Western Hemisphere was the German edition, published in 1743 by Christoph Sauer. Curiously enough, the first German books in America were printed by no less a person than Benjamin Franklin. When he was asked by the English Parliament how many Germans there were in Pennsylvania, he answered, "About one third of the whole population." The legislature of Pennsylvania, in its minutes of 1789–1790, ordered all important laws enacted during its session to be published in German as well as English.

The earlier immigrants came largely because of religious difficulties in the Old World. When these had subsided, few Germans came over. With the revolutions of 1830 and 1848, emigration was resumed. Large numbers of peasants and mechanics came over who settled in various parts of the country. The second wave included a good many political intellectuals who called themselves the "Forty-Eighters." They favored the Midwest, particularly Missouri, where some planned to establish the type of liberal community they had not realized in Germany. The most distinguished of the Forty-Eighters was the idealistic Carl Schurz, who became Secretary of the Interior and Minister to Spain. His wife was largely responsible for the introduction of the kindergarten in the United States.

The Forty-Eighters were, on the whole, highly cultured. They sought to maintain the German language and founded elementary and secondary schools which became model educational institutions. In fact, they were superior to, and in some communities outnumbered the public schools. The latter, in order to draw pupils to their classes, also introduced German. That language became so firmly rooted that in 1903 the United States Commissioner of Education in his report commented, "The German language has actually become the second language of our Republic." In the Midwest there were twice as many pupils enrolled in German classes as in French. The largest enrollments were in San Francisco, Denver, St. Louis, Milwaukee, Cincinnati, Chicago, Cleveland, Buffalo, Baltimore, and New York.

German, then, was the first modern language to establish itself in the American curriculum. Not only was it widely taught but excellent texts were provided. Teacher training institutes were maintained and professional literature was published.

The outbreak of the First World War caused a sharp decline in German enrollments. In fact, the language received so severe a blow that it has never recovered. Emotions ran high. In the city of New York the high school enrollment in German—which had been the leading language—dropped from 25,000 to a mere 40 students, and these 40 were in one high school.

The status and development of French in the United States have been quite different. French could never rely for influence on the number of its native speakers, for they have always been few. Frenchmen are loath to emigrate from *la belle France.* Still, because of its traditional prestige in Europe, and because of the close bonds of friendship between the United States and France, it has always maintained itself here as the language of culture and refinement. As mentioned above, it was taught in the Colonies in the earliest times. It was part of the curriculum of the academies, and later of the high schools. Enrollments in French classes were particularly strong in New England and in the South during the nineteenth century. In the Midwest it was outstripped by German until 1918.

Spanish was not taught to any extent until the outbreak of the Spanish-American War. With the entrance of the United States upon the Latin-American scene, interest in the language of our neighbors was aroused. The acquisition of Puerto Rico made a Spanish-speaking island part of the United States. Our rapidly growing trade with South America brought about a demand for personnel equipped with Spanish. The Good Neighbor Policy and the activities of the Pan-American Union increased the interest in the language and culture of South America.

With the drop in German in 1917 due to the war hysteria, French and Spanish enrollments grew by leaps and bounds. French led for a while, but was at length overtaken by Spanish.

Not that Spanish was warmly received. Quite the contrary. For the longest time teachers of French and German looked down upon Spanish as an interloper. They sometimes spoke of it disparagingly as an inferior language without any important literature. The position of Spanish was weakened by the fact that thousands of teachers of German, having lost their pupils, by force of circumstances became unwilling instructors in the newly arrived language. Furthermore, unlike French and German, there were no trained Spanish language teachers, no well-organized methods, courses, or carefully edited textbooks. Only with the years, as increasing numbers of Hispanists were trained, was Spanish able to catch up in this respect. Then it captured the market because of its alleged ease and because of the supposed vocational opportunities.

"Spanish is easy" and "Spanish for business" were the slogans. Strangely enough, Hispanists considered these disparaging reflections on their subject and rejected them with anger. Actually, both statements are fundamentally true and both have helped to increase Spanish enrollments. As modern languages go, Spanish, because of its regularity, its almost phonetic spelling, and its ease of pronunciation, is certainly less difficult to acquire than an inflected language like German or Latin. And it does offer, by far, the best vocational opportunities of any of the languages taught in our schools. Every Sunday in one of New York's leading newspapers there are over one hundred want ads calling for competence in a foreign language, and over 80 per cent of the requests are for

Spanish. We do have a huge volume of trade with Latin America.

It is interesting to note that French, German, Italian, and Spanish—the languages now most widely taught throughout the country—were the very ones offered in Colonial institutes of learning. Benjamin Franklin recommended them for his Academy in Philadelphia (which later became the University of Pennsylvania). Thomas Jefferson helped to establish the first modern language department at the College of William and Mary, which offered the same four languages.

Italian did not at any time become as widespread as French or German. Even now it is concentrated in larger metropolitan areas, although numerically Italo-Americans are, next to the German-speaking groups, the largest non-English speaking stock in the country.

In view of this steady stream of immigration—which has not yet ceased—one may say that the United States is a nation of immigrants. All these people brought their own language and culture to America. Some came because of religious persecution, some to escape military service, others to better their economic condition. Many were imbued with high social and political ideals and looked to America as the utopia where they would find peace and happiness in a near-perfect society. The invitation inscribed on the base of the Statue of Liberty promised a cordial welcome:

> Give me your tired, your poor,
> Your huddled masses yearning to breathe free,
> The wretched refuse of your teeming shore,
> Send these, the homeless, tempest-tossed, to me;
> I lift my lamp beside the golden door.

The immigrants soon discovered, however, that they were not welcome. Each succeeding wave of new arrivals—Irish, Germans, Italians, Russian and Polish Jews—encountered coldness, prejudice, hostility. The foreigner was forced to live among his own people since he was rejected by the American community. This led to the establishment of foreign-speaking settlements. Not only were there foreign quarters in the larger cities; entire towns were populated by one ethnic group. A classic example of this is Egg Harbor City, New Jersey, where newspapers, church services, and even the town records were maintained in German for fifty years.

Two tendencies manifested themselves among the immigrants. One was to adjust as rapidly as possible to the new environment; the other was to preserve their cultural heritage. The former process was hastened by economic need, by ridicule heaped on him for his foreign speech and manners, and by high-pressure Americanization programs.

And so within a short time the laborer, mechanic, and tradesman of foreign origin sloughed off his native culture, forgot his mother tongue, and became an American. Sometimes he even changed his name. The "melting pot" had done its work. This process was so rapid and so thorough that it was not appreciated by European historians and sociologists. When they visited America they viewed with amazement the large numbers of Germans, Italians, Austrians, Scandinavians, and Slavs who had retained their foreign patronymics and physiognomies, but were unable to say anything in what was once their native tongue.

The more cultured members of the various ethnic groups were alarmed at this tendency and tried to stem the tide. They endeavored to preserve their native culture and mother tongue by founding societies, publishing magazines and newspapers, and establishing private schools. They were especially successful in their efforts in the larger urban centers, where there were considerable concentrations of foreign-born groups. This is true of New York City, where there are private schools in French, German, Greek, Magyar, Danish, Czech, Chinese, and Yiddish. These are by no means all small or obscure enterprises. The French maintain a full-fledged *lycée* of 700 students and turn away hundreds of applicants owing to lack of space. The Germans have a society which supports several schools enrolling about 600 pupils. The Chinese school is attended every afternoon by some 400 children. A Jewish workmen's group maintains 40 schools in which Yiddish is taught.

The number of American newspapers in foreign languages has declined somewhat. At the turn of the century there were published in New York daily papers in Yiddish (4), German (5), Italian, French, Greek, Polish, Russian, and Spanish. There is at least one paper in each of these languages at this time. Because of the changes in ethnic composition, Yiddish and German have declined in numbers, whereas there has been a great increase in Spanish. Throughout the country there are over 80 foreign-language dailies and 600 periodicals in almost 50 languages.

Daily radio programs are offered in the foreign languages mentioned. Also motion pictures and stage plays are given in French, German, Italian, and Spanish. In New York there are now many movie houses that offer only Spanish-spoken films.

Spanish has reached such proportions that one might say that New York is a bilingual city. Special courses have been set up to train police officers, nurses, social workers, judges, prison wardens, and other municipal employees in that language. Sanitation and driving regulations are issued in Spanish. The recent (1960) census blank was also produced in a Spanish version. All this is evidence of the fact that America is still—and in certain sections very much—multilingual.

In view of this, and because of the present urgent need for linguists in international relations, it is deplorable that the immigrants to America during the past century were in such a hurry to drop their mother tongues. That was a distinct cultural loss. If a considerable portion of these millions had held on to their languages, today's average American would have grown up to be bilingual. This would have been a great economic as well as cultural asset in a world of many languages and rival ideologies. As it is, we are now forced to recover painfully what we could have had without effort.

But what have our schools and colleges done in this respect? Have they taught foreign languages effectively?

2 · The U.S. Is Caught Short

LANGUAGES FOR LEISURE—IF AT ALL

FOR centuries Latin and Greek had been the major subjects in the secondary schools of Europe. They still play an important role in the *Gymnasium* and the *lycée*. This tradition was transferred to America where it was maintained in the academies. It is preserved in the very name of so renowned an institution as the Boston Latin School.

Although introduced by Benjamin Franklin in his Academy in Philadelphia before the Revolution, the modern languages came in slowly. The teachers of the classics viewed them with disdain; the universities were loath to grant credits for them.

Not until 1883, were the modern language teachers influential and numerous enough to organize on a national basis. It was then that the Modern Language Association came into being. The classical languages, however, held their own. As late as 1895, over 43 per cent of all students in public high schools were enrolled in Latin courses and only 17 per cent in modern languages. Over the years Latin declined steadily, and by 1955 the enrollments had sunk to less than 7 per cent. The modern languages, however, had also gone down since the all-time high of 50 per cent in 1900. In 1955 they enrolled only 13.7 per cent of the high school population.

The colleges and universities in their earliest days were

citadels of classical learning. Only Latin, Greek, and Hebrew were acceptable; modern languages were frowned upon. In fact, they were not admitted to the leading institutions—Harvard, Yale, Pennsylvania University, Princeton, William and Mary, Columbia, and Williams—until the middle of the eighteenth century. Study of the living languages was not considered regular college work and in the beginning no academic credit was given for their pursuit. The teachers were hired tutors who were not officially members of the staff.

Gradually, changes were brought about. A professorship in German had been established as early as 1754 at the University of Pennsylvania. In 1779, the first modern language department was organized at William and Mary. And in 1825, George Ticknor was named professor of French and Spanish at Harvard. In the same year Longfellow, who succeeded Ticknor at Harvard, became professor of French, German, Italian, and Spanish at Bowdoin. He had traveled widely in Europe and had done some excellent translations of verse from the Scandinavian languages, from French, German, Italian, Spanish, Latin, and Portuguese. With consummate wisdom he imported natives to teach the languages to his students, so that their accent might be as nearly perfect as possible, while he, the professor, conducted the courses in literature.

George Ticknor was a unique personality and one of our earliest scholars. Together with a number of other distinguished New Englanders, he journeyed to the University of Göttingen in Hanover, which enjoyed a reputation for a new type of scholarship. Ticknor's companions were deeply impressed with German research and remained at Göttingen. Ticknor, however, went to Spain, immersed himself in Spanish literature, and became the first great American Hispanist. His *History of Spanish Literature* is still a valuable reference work.

Latin and Greek had been considered "disciplines"—subjects to be pursued because they trained the mind and prepared for college. No one claimed that they had any "practical value." As one English schoolmaster put it proudly when a member of an educational commission asked him, "What is the value of Latin?"—"Thank God, it has no value!"

In its elementary form Latin was a mental discipline; on its higher level it introduced the student to Roman literature and culture. Acquaintance with the latter was part of the cultural equipment of every well-educated gentleman. It had little relationship to daily life.

When the modern languages were introduced they followed in the path of Latin. The aims and methods of the classical languages were taken over by the teachers of French and German. No attempt was made to be practical. In the case of the student with a teaching career in view, language study meant research in philology or literature. In the case of the general student, it meant a certain amount of reading in the foreign language, preparing him for a life of *otium cum dignitate,* in the words of Cicero—"cultured leisure."

It was no wonder, then, that when the high school doors were opened to *hoi polloi,* the atmosphere changed. Formerly, only the upper 15 per cent of elementary school pupils had gone on to high school; now everyone was to get a secondary education. It was discovered very soon that a considerable percentage of the new arrivals were "non-academically-minded." But the school was there to give them an education; educable or not, they had to be provided for. And so educational experts and curriculum makers scurried about to make the educational pabulum palatable to the pupil. Essentially this meant simplifying the difficult subjects. The watered-down versions were called "general." And thus came into being General Mathematics, General Science, and General Language. The latter was primarily a sampling of a number of languages which gave the student a bare smattering of four or five and competence in none. In some cases it was used for prognostic purposes, i.e., to determine whether the student possessed any linguistic aptitude; in others it was "exploratory," which meant that the student was to choose one of the languages for continued study.

By this time many of the teachers of foreign languages had been intimidated. Even their leaders lost heart. Between 1925–1928 a nation-wide survey was made under the auspices of the National Foreign Language Study. In the final report, known after the chairman of the committee as the "Coleman Report," the reading aim was recommended. This, it was felt, was the only feasible objective to set up for the two years of study given by most students to a foreign language. The situation seemed so hopeless that even those who took a dim view of the reading aim, made no attempt to demand an extension of the course and a greater emphasis on speaking the language.

Foreign languages lost ground rapidly and were viewed with contempt by school administrators. Some of the more extreme curriculum-makers were ready to drop them altogether. The various reports issued at intervals by committees of educators on the aims and the scope of American education gave less and less space to the area, if they mentioned it at all.

A committee of the American Youth Commission issued a report in 1940, entitled "What the High Schools Ought to Teach." Foreign language courses were condemned as useless and time-consuming. If there must be language instruction, said the report, let it be General Language.

Four years later the Educational Policies Commission of the National Education Association published *Education for All American Youth.* It allowed a niggardly two hours out of 20 in the week's program for foreign languages. Those who lived on the farm or in the village, might, if they were eager to learn a foreign language, take a correspondence course. *O tempora, O mores!*

The apogee of the ludicrous, however, was reached by a group of distinguished scholars at Harvard. After laboring for three years, twelve august professors and 60 specialists brought forth a report which recommended a core curriculum sans languages. In the 13 pages of *General Education in a Free Society* devoted to foreign languages (the section is under "English"), the following brilliant thoughts are expressed:

Foreign language study is useful primarily in strengthening the student's English. Translation is excellent practice. For the average student there is no real need at all to learn a foreign language. Continued language study should be provided only for the "relatively few" who are interested or competent. Russian and Ancient Greek have peculiar values and are therefore recommended for the high school. Anyway, all the alleged benefits of foreign language study can be derived from a course in General Language. And as for vocational competence, all an engineer has to do, who finds he needs a language, is to take a summer course to acquire sufficient facility in the tongue. This from our most venerable and most revered citadel of scholarship!

Another height of the ludicrous was reached in the Life Adjustment Report which came out of Washington. The authors of this brilliant document, sponsored by the United States Office of Education, were particularly concerned with the 30 per cent who did not fit into the high school—even after core curricula, General Science, and art weaving had been introduced. And so, willy nilly, the high school had to be fitted to them. The solution of the experts was to give the pupil what he liked and what he could do successfully—wood-carving, clay modeling, water colors, photography, checkers, stamp collecting, etc. The program sounds like that of a summer camp for small children. Cognitive learning was practically eliminated.

One can hardly believe that serious-minded educational experts could write such stuff. In the brochure of 421 pages entitled *Education for All American Youth,* a bare mention is made of "languages" exactly five times. They are never discussed; only once are six modern languages mentioned by name. The authors say that it might be "feared" "quite mistakenly" . . . "that this course would put an end to the systematic study of bodies of knowledge," but, they assure the perturbed reader, there is "ample time in the total school program for any student who wishes" to pursue an academic subject. Correspondence courses are recommended; they have proved successful in foreign languages, photography, radio, forestry, aeronautics, and astronomy! Incidentally, many of the bulletins on life adjustment education are devoted to hobbies, dancing, dating, and mating.

An educational philosophy like this had little room for foreign languages. They continued to decline. In 1928, over 25 per cent of the high school population was enrolled in language study; 25 years later it had dropped to almost half of that.

It seemed impossible to stem the tide of anti-intellectualism in American education. What could the despised teacher of Latin, French, or German do in the face of bulletins issued under the aegis of the Office of Education? Who would listen to his feeble voice as against the thundering pronouncements of professors and educationists?

A RUDE AWAKENING

The result of this disparagement of foreign language study over the years, the shortening and weakening of courses, and the acceptance of the reading aim soon became obvious. A generation of Americans had gone through high school and college without acquiring command of a foreign language.

The shock came when the Army urgently needed officers and men in Europe with linguistic competence and discovered that very few could handle even the simplest French and German. What had these young men done in their language courses, was the question.

In the case of Japanese, the urgency was greater and the available competence even less. In fact, it was negligible. In December, 1940 the Navy could discover only 12 officers among its personnel of 200,000 men who could be considered competent in the use of spoken and written Japanese. In view of the possibility of war with Japan, this lack of linguistically equipped personnel was ominous. Steps were taken at once to organize intensive training courses for officers.

A survey undertaken from March to June in 1941 revealed a pathetic lack of civilians who knew any Japanese. In the entire country only 56 Americans between 20 and 35 years of age could be found who knew enough Japanese to warrant further training!

This was bad enough. Another shock, however, came when the institutions of higher learning were called upon to help out. Because of the lack of suitable facilities and the requisite curriculum in the various colleges and universities where Japanese and Chinese were taught, the Navy decided to set up its own courses.

The Army Specialized Training Program (A.S.T.P.) was set up in a number of colleges where selected students were taught intensively. The American teacher was aided by an "informant" who was a native speaker of the language. Mechanical devices such as phonograph records, films, and motion pictures were used. Within 9 months the students emerged, capable of carrying on an ordinary conversation in situations that might confront them as soldiers in a foreign country.

The apparent success of the A.S.T.P. was widely publicized. The question was frequently asked: Why can't the schools do as well? The answer was a simple one: the schools did not operate under the same favorable conditions as the A.S.T.P.

Essentially these were as follows:

1. The small class size. Students in the A.S.T.P. met in groups of a dozen or less.

2. The singleness of aim. The objective was to provide the young men with fluency in everyday, practical expressions needed in the foreign country.

3. The selected student body. Only intelligent and eager young men were admitted to the course. Many of them already had a good foundation in the language.

4. The excellent motivation. Proficiency was rewarded, failure punished. Those who did not maintain a certain grade were not given week-end passes. Graduates of the course looked forward to advancement.

5. The intensive method. Continued, concentrated practice on a limited amount of subject matter could not fail to achieve rapid learning.

6. The use of mechanical equipment. Generous use was made of audio-visual aids.

7. The employment of natives. In addition to the American teacher, use was made of a foreign assistant or informant who spoke no English to the students.

8. The generous allotment of time. Each student received 17 hours of instruction weekly. In addition, there were many hours of practice and drill.

9. The absence of competition of other subjects. The student confined his efforts solely to the acquisition of a speaking knowledge of a given foreign language. He did not have to divide his energies among a number of subjects.

With such a highly concentrated and intensive program, success in the aim set was assured. Under similar conditions the school could do equally well. However, a language course set up in this way would not be desirable, since the school is an educational institution with essentially cultural aims and not an Army camp drilling young men to meet a highly specialized situation.

A committee of the American Council on Education that made a detailed study of the A.S.T.P. concluded that the courses were not continued long enough "to show conclusively the soundness and validity of the program for post-war education."

There is an anecdote to the effect that some of the men trained in Norwegian were sent to North Africa and men rarin' to use their Arabic found themselves in Iceland. When a concerned observer queried Washington about this, the reply was: "Oh, that was done to fool the enemy!"

Although it was not possible to evaluate the effectiveness of the Army method, it was undoubtedly the most intensive program of foreign language instruction ever attempted in the United States. It did have some beneficial influence on teaching in the schools and colleges, for it focused attention on the importance of (1) small classes, (2) the use of audio-visual devices, (3) singleness of aim, (4) practice in speaking, and (5) a high degree of motivation.

It stimulated the production of phonograph records for instructional purposes for class use. Heretofore they had been intended solely for the adult seated at home beside his lamp. Reading was rejected; there was clamor for the spoken language. A cry arose for "conversation." Literary selections were replaced in textbooks by dialogues taking place in restaurants, hotels, railroad stations, and the barber shop. The student no longer read stories by Daudet or wrote compositions on the life of Pasteur; he queried his way to the hotel, the postoffice, and the bathroom.

Although the A.S.T.P. was primarily an Army project, public interest in the teaching and learning of foreign languages was definitely increasing. This was due in part to activities supported by the United Nations Educational, Scientific and Cultural Organization, commonly known as UNESCO. Through its efforts the U.S. Commission for UNESCO was established in July, 1946 to advise the government and to act as liaison between the American public and UNESCO. An outgrowth of this was the Citizens' Consultation Groups, whose purpose was to discuss the proposition: Is the national interest served by the increased study of foreign languages, and if so, what sort of study would serve the country and the individual best?

At the request of the National Commission, a brochure entitled *The National Interest and Foreign Languages* was prepared by Professor William R. Parker, a member of the Commission and formerly Executive Secretary of the Modern Language Association of America. The first edition was published in April, 1954; a revised edition with much new material appeared in January, 1957. This "work paper" was to serve as a discussion guide for Citizens' Consultation Groups all over the country.

In August, 1953, UNESCO sponsored an International Seminar on the Teaching of Modern Languages in Ceylon. This resulted in a comprehensive report. Also, a number of sessions of the U.S. National Commission for UNESCO were devoted to a discussion of foreign language study.

All this was very encouraging, but it left the situation—as so frequently is the case in educational questions—in the realm of conference, discussion, recommendations, and reports. Had anything changed in the classroom? Had anything been done within the walls of the school to extend or improve the teaching of foreign languages?

For some time in a number of smaller communities a foreign language had been taught in the lower grades of the elementary school. This was not generally known; in fact, even language teachers as a whole were not aware of it. The most ardent champion of the project was Professor Theodore Andersson of Yale, who presented his ideas in a brochure entitled *The Teaching of Foreign Languages in the Elementary School,* published by D. C. Heath & Co. in 1953. Successful classes in the lower grades had been conducted in New England by James H. Grew of Phillips Academy, Andover, Mass., and Dr. Arthur M. Selvi of the Teachers College in New Britain, Conn.

The major contention of the protagonists of language in the grade schools was that the great weakness in our language teaching was that children did not begin their study of a foreign tongue until they were too old to learn it in a natural way. They maintained that the lower grades were the ideal place to teach a foreign language, for (1) the young child is without the inhibitions of the older student, (2) his speech organs are still flexible and he will have no difficulty in learning foreign sounds, (3) since he is a child, he learns the foreign language like his own mother tongue, and (4) an early start is absolutely necessary for language mastery, since acquiring facility in a language requires years of practice.

These ideas received a strong impetus through a speech made in St. Louis in May, 1952 by Dr. Earl J. McGrath, United States Commissioner of Education, in which he warmly recommended foreign language teaching in the grade schools. It aroused country-wide attention and almost immediately a movement, later called FLES (Foreign Languages in Elementary Schools), developed and gathered startling momentum. Within a few years 300,000 grade school children were receiving instruction in a foreign language. The figure now given is 700,000.

The movement was also strengthened and supported by a grant of the Rockefeller Foundation to the Modern Language Association for the purpose of making a thorough study of the teaching of foreign languages in the United States.

FLES is now well established in many parts of the country, although several basic problems remain to be solved. One of the chief ones is, in what grade is instruction to begin? Another is, what languages are to be offered? And a third is, are the teachers to be specialists, or regular grade teachers?

Despite the enthusiasm over FLES and the public interest in learning to speak a foreign language—reflected in the increased enrollments in private language schools and the huge sale of phonograph records—there was no essential change in the basic organization of language courses in high schools and colleges. The high school student still pursued his two years of French or Spanish. Extremely few students got into the third and fourth years. Language study remained an elective.

Then something happened which startled the entire world and shocked our political and educational leaders into action. That was the launching of Sputnik in the fall of 1957 by the Soviets. The fact that this event was so unexpected was in itself a sad reflection of the ignorance of our scientists about the activities of their Soviet colleagues, and revealed their inability to read scientific abstracts in Russian. Had any of them possessed that ability, they would have been able to read the announcement of Sputnik *five months earlier!* It was a classic example of how our national safety is jeopardized by the lack of personnel trained in foreign languages.

America was roused from its self-complacency; it was evident that the Russians not only ranted, boasted, and exaggerated but were also able to produce the goods. Consternation seized some of our international specialists. Experts dashed to Moscow to look into the science and educational system of the Soviets. Committees of educators visited Russian schools. The number of American tourists visiting Russia increased enormously; in response, the Soviets obligingly dropped most of their restrictions and provided eager and polite guides who spoke perfect English. This was, of course, a great help to the Americans, very few of whom knew any Russian.

Reports were issued, scores of articles were written. Some observers scoffed, others praised, but all were ready to admit that we were facing a formidable rival with whom we could not afford to trifle. Something had to be done.

There were those who were ready to scrap American educational ideals and imitate the Russians. Others, more coolheaded, suggested that we immediately set to work to improve our educational system. In comparing it with that of the Soviets ours seemed to be weakest in science, mathematics, and foreign languages. With reference to the latter, the striking fact was that in the Soviet Union millions of children in the middle school were learning English, whereas there were fewer than ten high schools and only a small number of colleges in the United States that offered Russian courses. The high school program in mathematics and science was much stronger there, too, if only because more time was put in by the Russian student. Ivan goes to school six days a week; he has six hours daily, plus extracurricular activities, and two hours of homework.

The thinking went beyond a survey of the schools of the Soviets. It was a period of worried self-examination.

What was revealed?

First, that a foreign language competence which we could have had as a cultural heritage had been lost through neglect and indifference; second, that we were way behind other nations in foreign language instruction; third, that we lived in a world in which, in vast areas, other languages were more widely spoken than our own; and fourth, that our efforts to meet the Soviet challenge were still halting, faltering, and inept.

Let us examine these points in detail.

3 · We Are at the Bottom

FOREIGN LANGUAGES—THE STRONGEST SUBJECT IN FOREIGN SCHOOLS

As has been pointed out previously, the study of foreign languages occupies the weakest position of any major subject in the American high school curriculum. Almost half our public high schools offer no instruction in a foreign language. Less than a fifth of the high school population takes a foreign language and then, in most cases, for only two years.

A comparison of our offerings with the curricula of other nations reveals an astounding, a pathetic backwardness in this area. Except possibly for other English-speaking countries, the leaders of no foreign school system consider a secondary education complete without the study of at least one foreign language for a number of years. In many countries more than one foreign language is required. All give language instruction a major position in the curriculum.

The language taught varies, of course, with the geographic location and the commercial and cultural contacts of a given country. In general, however, in European schools, English, French, and German play a dominant role. It is also interesting to note how prevalent is the teaching of Latin. In the classical course of Continental schools Greek is also required.

The Second World War caused a number of revisions. In

many systems English replaced French as the leading modern language. In some instances, German has been given less emphasis. Also, Russian has been introduced in a number of school systems.

Let us take a look at the language program of some of the leading foreign countries.

Austria

The *Mittelschule* (approximately, ages 10–18) comprises four types: the *Gymnasium,* the *Realgymnasium,* the *Realschule* and the *Frauenoberschule.*

With reference to languages, the curriculum of the *Mittelschule* is as follows (hours per week):

LOWER DIVISION

	I	*II*	*III*	*IV*
First modern language (English or French)	5	4	4	4
Latin			5	5

Under the Occupation, Russian was included as a required subject. Now it is an elective.

UPPER DIVISION

Gymnasium	*V*	*VI*	*VII*	*VIII*
Greek	5	5	6	6
Latin	4	4	6	6
First modern language	2	2		
Realgymnasium				
First modern language	2	2	2	2
Second modern language (French, Italian, Russian)	5	5	3	3
Latin	4	4	6	6
Realschule				
First modern language	2	2	2	2
Second modern language	3	3	2	2

In the Austrian curriculum more hours are devoted to modern languages than any other subject. In the seventh year of the *Realgymnasium* 11 hours out of 31 are allotted to foreign languages. This does not include German, the national language.

Denmark

The number of hours per week of instruction in foreign languages is as follows in the various types of schools:

THEORETICAL MIDDLE SCHOOL

	I	*II*	*III*	*IV*
German		5	4	4
English	6	3	3	3
Danish (for comparison)	5	4	4	5

Only mathematics gets as much time as foreign languages, which occupy about one fifth of the weekly program. In grade III, out of 35 hours, 7 are allotted to two foreign languages.

FOUR YEAR PREPARATORY SCHOOL

	I	*II*	*III*	*IV*
English	4	4	4	4
French			2	3
German	4	4	4	4

As seen above, in the fourth year 11 hours are given over to foreign languages. The next largest time allotment is to mathematics, which gets 7 hours per week in year IV.

FIVE YEAR PREPARATORY SCHOOL

	I	*II*	*III*	*IV*	*V*
English	5	3	3	4	4
French				2	3
German		5	4	4	4

In the fifth year 11 hours out of 30 are devoted to modern languages.

THREE YEAR "GYMNASIUM"

Classical Side	*I*	*II*	*III*
English and/or German	3	3	
French	4	4	4
Greek	6	6	6
Latin	5	5	6

In I and II, out of 36 hours, foreign languages get 18 hours. Of these, 11 are in Latin and Greek.

Modern Language Side			
Danish (given for comparison)	4	4	4
English	5	5	5
French	4	4	4
German	4	4	4
Latin	4	4	3

The above shows that every student in this division takes three modern languages and one ancient language. In I and II, out of 36 hours 17 are devoted to foreign languages, which is almost half.

Science Side			
Danish (given for comparison)	4	4	4
English and/or German	3	3	
French	4	4	4

Out of 36 hours, modern languages get 7. In other words, even in the science course almost one fifth of the time is devoted to language study.

France

The 7 years of secondary education end with the so-called *baccalauréat* examination. All students are required to study one modern language throughout the 7 years of the *lycée*. In their third year they begin Greek or a second modern language, which they continue to study for 4 years. The languages offered are English, German, Spanish, Italian, Russian, and Arabic.

In the *classique* section Latin is compulsory; in the *moderne* section it is not required.

In the first 2 years a foreign language is studied 3 hours a week in the *classique* and 5 hours a week in the *moderne.* In the remaining years the time allotment is 3 hours, except in the final class where it is 1½ hours. The second language gets 3 hours in the third year, 4 hours in the fourth, fifth and sixth, and 1½ hours in the seventh.

In the *cours complémentaires*—about equivalent to the American high school—4 years of general education are offered. All students study a modern language, 5 periods during the first 2 years and 4 periods a week during the remaining 2 years. Foreign language study gets about one sixth of the total of 27 weekly periods.

In the business section of the technical high schools, a modern language is studied throughout. There, too, about one sixth of the time is devoted to language instruction. The recent reforms in the French educational system provide for an increase in foreign language instruction in all types of schools.

West Germany

Germany has always maintained a strong program in foreign language instruction.

Each of the 10 *Länder* maintains its own school system. The general plan is 8–9 years of elementary school (*Volksschule*) and various types of secondary schools called *Gymnasium, Realgymnasium, Oberrealschule* and *Aufbauschule.* The first 4 grades of the elementary school are known as *Grundschule.*

In all 10 *Länder* instruction in a foreign language is given in the elementary school from the fifth grade on. In 8 *Länder* it is English, in 2 it is French. In Hamburg and Bremerhaven English is a required subject for all. West Berlin offers not only English, but also French, Russian, and Latin.

A second foreign language is begun in the seventh grade; it may be either French, Latin, or English.

Secondary education, which follows upon the *Grundschule,* continues for 8 to 9 years. Two foreign languages are studied throughout the course, the choice depending upon the type of school. In the classical *Gymnasium* the emphasis is on Latin and Greek. In the *Realgymnasium* 2 foreign languages are pursued, generally English and Latin. The *Oberrealschule,* which stresses science, requires 2 modern languages. In the *Aufbauschule,* most students take English as a first language and Latin as a second.

Ireland (Eire)

Below are given the "recognized pupils subjects" (languages only), with the marks assigned.

	Junior	*Senior*
English	200	400
French	300	300
Gaelic (*Gaedhilg*)	300	600
German	300	300
Greek	400	400
Italian	300	300
Latin	400	400
Spanish	300	300

Significant is the fact that 7 foreign languages are offered; also the heavy weight given to the classical languages. In order to get his secondary school diploma, a student must pass 5 subjects which must include Irish and at least two subjects from the following: English, French, German, Italian, Latin, Spanish, history, geography, mathematics, and science.

Italy

In the second and third years of the *Scuola Media,* 3 hours a week are devoted to a foreign language, out of a total of 31 hours.

Two Year "Ginnasio"

	IV	V
Modern language	4	4
Greek	4	4
Latin	5	5

In the fifth year 13 out of a total of 27 hours, that is almost half, are given to foreign languages.

Three Year Classical "Ginnasio"

	I	II	III
Greek	3	3	3
Latin	4	4	4

Out of a total of 29 hours, 7 are allotted to languages.

Netherlands

There are 3 types of secondary institutions that prepare for higher education or for a career. The 6-year school provides 2 programs, Alpha and Beta. The first stresses languages, the second mathematics.

Alpha	*I*	*II*	*III*	*IV*	*V*	*VI*
Dutch	4	3	3	3	2	3
English		3	2	2	2	2
French	4	3	3	2	2	2
German			3	2	2	2
Greek		5	5	5	6	8
Latin	7	5	5	5	7	8

In the classical programs with Greek and Latin, foreign languages occupy almost two thirds of the curriculum. In III, for example, out of a total of 33 hours, 21 are devoted to foreign languages.

In *Beta,* the mathematics course, foreign language gets 18 hours out of 33 in year III.

Hogere Burgerschool

	I	II	III	IV	V
Dutch	4	4	4	4	4
English	3	3	3	4	4
French	5	3	3	4	4
German		3	3	4	4

(Dutch is included for the sake of comparison)

In III, out of a total of 33 hours, foreign language gets 9.

Norway

In the Folk High School, English is taught 3 hours weekly out of the 42.

In other types of Norwegian schools the picture is as follows:

	Three Year "Realskola"			Two Year "Realskola"	
	I	II	III	I	II
German	5	6		5	5
English	4	4	5	7	6

Nine Year Experimental Comprehensive School

	8th year	9th year
German	(5)	(5)
English	7	7

The total number of periods weekly is 37.

In the primary schools English is optional in the sixth and seventh years. It is given 5 periods a week.

The weekly allotment of periods to foreign languages throughout the entire educational system is as follows:

	I	II	III	IV	V	VI	VII	VIII	IX	X	XI	XII
English						5	5	4	4	5	7	8
German								5	6	4	4	–
French										4	6	7

On the average, then, 10 periods out of the total of 36 are given over to language study. In the teacher training institutions, Latin is required; electives are German, English, French, Russian, Greek.

Spain

INSTITUTO

	I	*II*	*III*	*IV*	*V*	*VI*	*VII*
English or German				3	3	3	
Greek					2	2	2
Italian or French	3	3	3				
Latin	5	5	5	5	5	4	4

Out of 24 hours in year V, 10 hours are given to languages. The *institutos* are national, state-endowed schools.

Sweden

As in most European countries, English, French, and German are the foreign languages taught. In some *gymnasiums* Spanish, Finnish, or Russian is offered.

In the seventh year of the *Folkskola* 4 hours of the weekly 36 are devoted to English.

In the secondary schools the picture is as follows:

THREE YEAR "REALSKOLA"

	I	*II*	*III*
English	4	4	3
German	5	5	5
French	·		(3)

The total number of hours of instruction weekly is 29. In other words, modern language instruction gets almost one third of the time.

FOUR YEAR "REALSKOLA"

	I	*II*	*III*	*IV*
English	6	4	4	4
German		6	4	5

Five Year "Realskola"

	I	II	III	IV	V
English	6	6	3	3	4
German			6	4	5

In the Four Year *Realskola* out of 39 hours, 19 go to modern languages.

Four Year "Gymnasium"

Reallinje	I	II	III	IV
English	3	3	3	4
French	3	3	3	3
German	3	3	2	2

Latinlinje	I	II	III	IV
English	3	3	2	2
French	3	3	2	2
German	3	3	2	2
Greek			7	7
Latin	6	6	6	6

In the *Reallinje,* 9 out of 37 hours are devoted to modern languages. In the *Latinlinje,* in the third year, 21 of the 37 hours are given to foreign languages, that is, almost 60 per cent.

Switzerland

The language used in school depends upon the canton in which it is located. The languages used are French, German, and Italian. Two national languages are compulsory. A third national language is usually included, or English, which is elective.

The upper level of the *Gymnasium* is divided into 3 sections: Humanities, Sciences, and Modern Languages. Three types of *matura* are granted: A, Latin and Greek; B, Latin and Modern Languages; C, Mathematics and Science.

There is considerable variety in school organization. In the

Realschule of Bern, during his 4 years, the student is required to take 15½ hours of French, 13½ hours of English or Italian. In addition, he may elect 6 hours of English or Italian, or 7 hours of Latin. In other words, a student must take, counting his native German, 3 languages and he may elect 2 more. (German is practically another language, for there is a marked difference between the literary *Hochdeutsch* and the vernacular Schwyzer-Dütsch.) Aside from German, the program provides for 42 hours of foreign language instruction out of a total of 164 hours. It is evident that the student devotes one fourth of his time to language study.

The division of the *Gymnasium* known as the *Literarschule* allots even a greater proportion of time to languages. There are 2 sections, classical languages and modern languages.

The hours per week given to language instruction are as follows:

(Class designations are in Latin and in reverse order; i.e., *Quarta, Tertia, Secunda, Prima.*)

	IV		*III*		*II*		*I*	
Required:	*CL*	*ML*	*CL*	*ML*	*CL*	*ML*	*CL*	*ML*
German	3	4	3	4	3	4	4	5
French	3	3	3	3	3	3	3	3
Latin	6	6	6	6	5	5	5	5
Greek	6		6		6		5	
English or Italian		4		4		4		4
Elective:								
Hebrew		1		1		1	1	
English						2	2	
Italian						2	2	

The above table shows that out of a total of 157 hours a student is required to devote 67 to languages, with the option of electing 4 or 6 hours more of a foreign language.

Even in the *Handelsschule,* the school of commerce, the

language requirements are considerable. The 3-year course demands 11 hours of French, 9 of English, and 8 of Italian. Three hours of Spanish is optional. In other words, over one fourth of the program consists of foreign language study.

U.S.S.R.

In 1958, a committee of 10 educators under the chairmanship of L. G. Derthick, United States Commissioner of Education, made a study of the schools of the Union of Soviet Socialist Republics. The report of the First Official U.S. Education Mission to the U.S.S.R., entitled *Soviet Commitment to Education,* includes the following statement regarding aspects of Soviet education that made favorable impressions: "The heavy emphasis and effectiveness of foreign language instruction at the pedagogical institutes and universities."

In the body of the report a section is devoted to foreign language instruction. There an equally favorable opinion is expressed of the foreign language instruction in the secondary schools. English, German, or French is required of every pupil. English is the most widely studied language.

The Soviet curriculum is rather rigid; a choice is permitted only with respect to a specific foreign language. Approximately 45 per cent choose English, 35 per cent German, and 20 per cent French. In the general school, pupils begin the study of a foreign language in grade 5, that is, at the age of 11, and continue it through grade 10. At the end of the tenth grade the student will have had 20 hours, by the week, of language instruction. This is more than the curriculum allots to geography, biology, physics, chemistry, drawing, or shop work. Equal with foreign languages is the time allotted to history and physical culture; only mathematics and Russian language get more time; the latter is fixed at 84 hours, the former at 60.

The diploma examination at the end of the middle school includes a test in the foreign language studied (English, German, or French). To make the pupils masters of these tongues, a number of schools have been organized in which the instruction in most subjects is given in one of these three languages.

The aim of the instruction in foreign languages is twofold: (1) to provide the student with an effective tool of oral communication, and (2) to make it possible for him to read and translate literary, scientific, and political material.

English, which is taught from the fifth grade on, is pursued by over 1,500,000 pupils. In the universities and higher schools a reading and speaking knowledge of English is required.

The academic student continues the study of his chosen foreign language at the university level. He may even take up a second one.

More significant, undoubtedly, are the experimental language schools, of which there are 17 in the larger cities of the Soviet Union. Of these, 8 are for English, 7 for German, and 2 for French. In these institutions the study of the language is begun in the second grade, when the child is 8 years old. From grade 5 on the instruction in geography, history, and literature is given in the foreign language. These schools are designed to produce graduates who will be thoroughly fluent in the foreign tongue.

In addition to these experimental schools, there are general schools in which Arabic, Chinese, Hindi, and other Oriental languages are taught. These institutions are usually near the border of the country whose language is being learned.

In the pedagogical institutes, that is, the teacher training colleges, 8 semester hours of foreign language study are required. In the case of candidates for the foreign language faculty, the requirement, which includes phonetics, methods, literature, and practice, totals 184 semester hours. A second foreign language is allotted 59 semester hours. Thus, even in the teachers' colleges foreign language study is strong.

It is evident from the preceding tabulations that throughout the world the average secondary school system requires from 5 to 9 years of study of a foreign language. Frequently a second language is required; in some instances the program includes a third language. In any case, languages occupy from one fourth to one half of the time of the student.

The only countries in which a foreign language is not required are: Ireland, Japan, Scotland, Australia, New Zealand, and the United States. It is significant that, with the exception of Japan, they are all English-speaking.

In length of time devoted to foreign language study, the picture is as follows:

10 years: Ceylon, Iraq
9 years: Egypt, West Germany
8 years: Austria, Jordan, Mexico, Thailand, Yugoslavia
7 years: France, Spain, Portugal, Turkey
6 years: Burma, Denmark, Dominican Republic, Greece, Ireland, Japan, Scotland, U.S.S.R., Uruguay
5 years: Australia, Netherlands, New Zealand, Sweden, England
4 years: Brazil, Finland, Honduras, Iceland, Italy
3 years: Argentina
2 years: United States

In other words, the United States is at the bottom.

FOREIGN LANGUAGES—THE WEAKEST SUBJECT IN UNITED STATES SCHOOLS

When one considers that the United States is the richest nation on earth and that public education has been glorified as one of the greatest of American achievements, it is disheartening to observe what is offered in the way of foreign language study. It seems unbelievable that in any statistical compilation of length of school time devoted to foreign languages our country should be at the bottom of the list. Countries like Ceylon and Iraq offer ten years of compulsory study in a foreign language; the best the U.S. can show are two years of elective study. In fact, except for the English-speaking countries, and Japan, all other nations make foreign languages a required subject.

Statistics for the United States in this field are dismal. More than 56 per cent of all public high schools in our country do not offer a modern foreign language at all. A little over 14 per cent of all our high school students study a foreign language.

Only 2 foreign languages, Spanish and French, are pursued by a large number of students. About 7.3 per cent are enrolled in the former and 5.6 per cent in the latter. Less than 1 per cent (0.8 per cent) are enrolled in German classes.

Other languages—Italian, Polish, Hebrew, Russian—are offered only in larger cities or in communities with a given ethnic background, such as Portuguese, Swedish, Norwegian, etc. Russian was introduced only a few years ago and there are now about a hundred high schools in which it is taught. The more exotic languages like Chinese, Arabic, and Hindi are not offered on the secondary level in any American school. Where there are larger concentrations of Chinese, as in New York and San Francisco, private schools are maintained for the teaching of this language to the children.

Private language schools, as has been pointed out, are maintained by foreign-speaking groups in many parts of the country. There are such schools teaching French, German, Czech, Hungarian, Polish, Yiddish, Modern Greek, and Hebrew. These private schools undoubtedly help to keep the languages of the various ethnic groups alive, but they do not influence the curricula or the methods of the public schools. The spokesmen of foreign-language groups are aware of this and are continually endeavoring to have their language introduced into city systems.

According to William Parker in *The National Interest and Foreign Languages,* the situation differs from region to region, with reference to the proportion of high schools in a state offering modern languages. It extends all the way from 100 per cent for several New England states to 4.4 for North Dakota. In other words, whereas in Connecticut, Maine, New Jersey, and Rhode Island all public high schools teach a modern language, not one high school in ten does so in the Dakotas, Iowa, and Nebraska.

The various states of the union may be grouped as follows with reference to the percentage of its public high schools in which a modern language is taught:

Per Cent	
100	Connecticut, Maine, New Jersey, Rhode Island
94.1–97.6	California, Massachusetts, New Hampshire, Delaware
80.1–88.3	Arizona, Vermont, New York, Virginia, North Carolina
66.7–75.5	Maryland, Nevada, Washington, D.C., New Mexico
45.3–64.7	South Carolina, Michigan, Wyoming, Illinois, Pennsylvania, Ohio, Colorado, Florida
26.2–42.4	Georgia, West Virginia, Texas, Oregon, Idaho, Utah, Louisiana, Tennessee
19.3–24.5	Indiana, Alabama, Minnesota, Missouri, Montana, Kentucky, Kansas
4.4–18.1	Mississippi, Arkansas, Oklahoma, Nebraska, Iowa, South Dakota, North Dakota

Among the languages, Spanish takes the lead. It is studied by 7.3 per cent of the total population of the public high schools. However, it has not increased recently. In 1949, the percentage was 8.2, in 1928 it was 9.4, and in 1922 it was 11.3. Here, too, regional differences are marked. In New Mexico the proportion is 21.8 per cent, in Arizona 20.5 per cent and in California 19.3 per cent. On the other hand, the percentage for Maine is 1, for North Dakota 1.2, and Mississippi 1.3. In 38 states a total of over 329,000 students in public high schools were studying Spanish.

French is at present studied by 5.6 per cent of the high school population. In 1949, it was 4.7 per cent; in 1922, it was 15.5 per cent. French is strongest in the northeastern part of the country and weakest in the South and Midwest. For Massachusetts the percentage is 19.7, for Rhode Island 19.5, for New Hampshire 16.9. On the other hand, for South Dakota it is 0.1, for Kansas 0.2, for North Dakota 0.5, for Oklahoma 0.6, for Nebraska 0.8, and for Alabama 0.9. In 38 states it was found that a total of 249,631 high school students were learning French.

Latin used to be the most widely taught foreign language in American high schools; it is now second in enrollment. About 6.9 per cent of secondary students study the language of the Romans. There has been a steady decline within recent years as shown by the following figures: 27.4 per cent in 1922, 19.5 in 1934, 7.8 in 1949. However, the enrollments in Latin are higher than those in modern languages combined in the public high schools of North and South Dakota, Indiana, Mississippi, Ohio, West Virginia, and Wisconsin. In 11 other states Latin enrollments exceed those in any single modern language.

German classes, as mentioned previously enroll only 0.8 per cent of the high school population. It is not taught in any public high school in Alabama, North Carolina, South Carolina, Florida, Mississippi, New Mexico, Tennessee, Vermont, and Wyoming. Not one American high school student in a hundred is studying German.

Also, as pointed out above, the other foreign languages offered in the high schools of some states have a negligible enrollment. Classical Greek is offered in Massachusetts, New York, and Pennsylvania. Swedish is taught in some Midwestern schools. Portuguese is limited to a few schools in Massachusetts and Rhode Island. Norwegian is offered in a few schools in Minnesota and in one high school in Brooklyn, N.Y. Polish is studied in Connecticut, Massachusetts, New Jersey, Ohio, and Pennsylvania. Its largest enrollment is, however, in Catholic parochial schools.

Hebrew has an enrollment of about 5,000 in New York. There are smaller enrollments in California, Massachusetts, Missouri, New Jersey, and Rhode Island.

Outside of New York and a number of other metropolitan areas, Italian does not have a very large enrollment.

One of the major reasons for the limited enrollments in Italian, Portuguese, Hebrew, and even German is the fact that so frequently the language has been introduced as a gesture to a local ethnic group interested in that particular language. The motivation is sentimental and emotional, rather than based on objective reasons. Any foreign language offered in a public high school should be taught because of its importance and value to all American students.

We have examined only the numbers of students enrolled and have found the picture disappointing. It is not brighter when we consider the courses offered and the amount of teacher preparation.

Not only is the learning of a modern language confined to less than 20 per cent of our high school students, but that learning does not extend beyond 2 years in most cases. This practice seemed to be so firmly fixed that the national committee of the Modern Foreign Language Study, after a nation-wide survey completed in 1928, made no attempt to change it. In fact, the committee set up the reading aim as the only feasible objective. It was recognized that it was impossible to acquire a speaking competence in a 2-year high school course.

No public high school offers a third year of any modern language in North Dakota, South Dakota, Idaho, Mississippi, or South Carolina. There is no fourth year in nine additional states.

On the other hand, the situation in private schools is much better. Over 7 million pupils attend public high schools; about 900,000 are in private or boarding schools. In the Catholic schools there has always been strong emphasis on Latin. The preparatory schools, in general, have a strong language program, since they are essentially academic institutions. A survey of 43 prep schools revealed standard programs of 4 years of French. One offered 6 years; 14 provided 5 years of instruction and 34 had 3 years.

In all of the public high schools foreign language is an elective subject. In addition to shortness of the course—2 years—there is another factor which prevents the student from achieving any actual skill or mastery in a foreign language. That is the hiatus between high school and college. Many students take their language during the first 2 years of high school and do nothing with it in their junior and senior years. By the time they enter college, they have forgotten a good deal. Only about half of our high school students go to college, but certainly provision should be made for them. The cessation of language study for a year or two is a fearful educational waste. The taking of a college placement test, later on, is frustrating and annoying.

The colleges have complained about the quality of language preparation in the high school, but have done nothing to overcome it. In fact, they have helped to weaken the status of foreign languages in the high schools by reducing their entrance requirements.

As pointed out in the previous section, a comparison of the length of our foreign language courses with that in other countries puts us at the bottom. This is the basic weakness of our program.

Fortunately, this has been recognized by our political and educational leaders. Many voices have been raised in protest. A change is definitely taking place. However, it is proceeding much too slowly. The international situation is critical. Time is of the essence.

How great the urgency is will be set forth in the following section.

4 · World Languages for World Contacts

A TONGUE-TIED LEADER

As an outgrowth of two wars, the United States has become the leader of the Western world, not only politically, but commercially and culturally. Uncle Sam is, however, a rather unhappy leader. He has had responsibilities thrust upon him which he did not ask for and for which he is not prepared.

Our country lacks the tradition of skillful diplomats and trained colonial administrators such as the European powers of the nineteenth century had. Furthermore, we are not confronted with vast areas populated by uncivilized peoples who can easily be trained (and exploited), but by dozens of recently liberated colonies trying to establish themselves as nations and clamoring for support. Eager to help, we have been generous with our money and technical aid. Unfortunately, we have lacked the major competence in dealing with foreign peoples, namely, an acquaintance with their culture and psychology. And this competence is quite impossible without a knowledge of their language.

And so Uncle Sam has continued with a smile handing out millions and millions of dollars and losing friends everywhere, much to his amazement. South America denounces "Yankee imperialism"; Cuba vilifies us; Panama is sullen. Our

European allies are lukewarm. China has definitely been lost; Korea is falling; Japan is wavering. The Arabic world is smoldering.

That this situation is due to inept diplomacy is obvious. How can diplomatic relations be carried on effectively, if they are conducted by men and women who have not been trained for this career?

The lack of such training in our diplomatic representatives has been appalling. A considerable number in the past have not even made an attempt to learn the language of the country in which they were stationed for years. There was the case of one of our ambassadors to a South American country who never learned more than "Buenos días" and "Sí, señor" in five years. How unreliable, costly, and dangerous it has been to rely on supposedly faithful interpreters is brought out drastically in the book, *The Ugly American.*

WORLD TRADE DEMANDS WORLD LANGUAGES

Since World War II there has been an enormous increase in our foreign trade. At the end of 1955, private investments abroad by American citizens had reached a total of 29 billion dollars, an increase of 2½ billion over the previous year. Over 12½ billions have been invested abroad by United States corporations since the end of the war. Our most extensive trade is with Latin America; it amounts to about 7 billion dollars a year. Half of this is export and half import. It represents more than 27 per rent of our imports and over 34 per cent of our exports.

In 1958, our exports amounted to almost 18 billion dollars and our imports to almost 15 billion. The leading countries to which our exports went, are, in descending order: Canada, Mexico, United Kingdom, Japan, Venezuela, Germany, Brazil, Italy, Netherlands, and France.

According to the Department of Commerce figures given in the *World Almanac,* our foreign trade with some of the more important countries in 1957 presented the following picture:

United States Foreign Trade with Leading Countries
(in millions of dollars)

	Exports	*Imports*
North and South America:		
Canada	$3,912.5	$2,906.9
20 American republics	4,567.3	3,764.4
Mexico	903.7	430.1
Central American republics	345.1	229.6
Cuba	618.0	481.9
Argentina	284.4	129.3
Brazil	484.4	699.7
Chile	194.9	195.8
Colombia	241.8	383.7
Peru	198.7	138.0
Venezuela	1,053.1	900.0
Western Europe:	5,697.1	3,077.5
Belgium and Luxembourg	419.7	270.4
France	589.3	256.0
West Germany	956.7	606.6
Italy	664.3	245.0
Netherlands	554.9	168.4
Sweden	231.8	118.7
Switzerland	238.8	173.2
Turkey	139.9	92.4
United Kingdom	1,110.9	765.7
Spain	203.7	58.3
Yugoslavia	144.0	35.4
Soviet bloc	86.1	61.3
Asia and Oceania:		
Western Asia	406.6	262.4
Iran	82.7	32.9
Israel	97.1	20.1
Saudi Arabia	68.9	41.0
Far East	3,248.2	1,938.4
India	439.3	210.9
Indonesia	110.2	200.3
Japan	1,234.0	600.5
Korea	277.5	3.9
Pakistan	115.4	39.6

	Exports	Imports
Asia and Oceania—(Continued)		
Philippines	369.3	262.1
Australia	212.6	146.9
Africa:	683.3	586.9
Belgian Congo	58.5	103.7
United Arab Republic	40.1	17.0
Liberia	59.6	38.3
Morocco	47.4	10.5
Union of South Africa	284.8	101.0

The total exports amounted to $20,850,300,000 and the total imports to $12,829,700,000.

This phenomenal growth in trade has created an urgent need for large numbers of people with foreign language equipment. In fact, for the concern selling its wares abroad it is a matter of efficiency and sound business practice to have a staff that can speak the language of the country in which they are stationed. We simply cannot compete with other nations if we rely on English alone.

World commerce is, next to our Foreign Service, the most vital area of our contact with other nations. The domination of the world is achieved more effectively—and far more humanely and less expensively—by the salesman than by the soldier. "World peace through world trade," the slogan of I.B.M., is an ideal well worth considering.

The number of our commercial contacts is continually expanding. According to the *Survey of Current Business,* there are almost a thousand American enterprises in Latin America with a total of 609,000 employees. Chiefly because of labor laws which require the hiring of a given percentage of natives, only 9,000 of this army of employees consists of Americans. However, they are the ones in the key positions; they are the ones that must have a competence in Spanish or Portuguese.

This competence must be a thorough one; it cannot be the superficial knowledge of a casual traveler or tourist. It always involves the technical vocabulary of the branch he is engaged in. He may be sent overseas on a specific assignment or commission. He may be a member of the staff who expects to live and work for a long time, perhaps for life, in the given foreign country. In any case, he is an emissary of American industry and a representative of the United States. His skill in the foreign language should be unusually good, for personal as well as for professional reasons.

Linguistic competence, of course, is secondary to technical knowledge of his field. Except for translating and interpreting, few jobs depend solely on knowledge of a language. In other words, an engineer who has acquired facility in Spanish gets his assignment in South America primarily because of his engineering skill.

As stated before, the competence in the foreign language should be a rather good one; it should go far beyond the ability to get along in everyday situations. The foreign representative of an American concern should be able to discuss the technical aspects of his field; he should be able to plan and to solve problems in the foreign language.

It is unnecessary to stress the fact that a knowledge of the customer's language has a distinct sales value. This is particularly true in Latin countries, where business conferences are conducted in a leisurely and unhurried way, in a highly social atmosphere. The American businessman who can speak the foreign tongue fluently and who can make intelligent comments on the art and literature of the country will gain not only the business but also the respect of the person he is dealing with.

Acquaintance with the historic and cultural background of the foreign people is a definite asset. If the representative of an American firm knows the psychology of the foreign people he is working with, he can deal far more effectively with problems of management, supervision, labor, and public relations. Without this knowledge he may unwittingly say and do things which run counter to the practices and thinking of the people with whom he is dealing.

A fluent command of the language will also vastly increase

the comfort and enjoyment of living in a foreign country. So often in the past Americans have held themselves aloof, segregating themselves in colonies which were miniature replicas of their home towns. Although they lived for years in a foreign country, they never made any friends among the natives and never learned anything about the foreign culture. They might just as well have stayed in the United States.

The importance as well as the value of competence in the foreign language for the American stationed abroad cannot be overstressed.

This is the way A. J. Vosskuhler, Manager of the Industrial Relations Department of the International Harvester Company expresses it:

> . . . the knowledge of a foreign language is an asset, but of minor consideration as it must be used in conjunction with a specialized trade or profession, such as documentation clerk, bilingual stenographer, diplomatic clerk, etc. These latter functions set the salary more so than the knowledge of a foreign language. . .

On the other hand, P. C. Sharp, Sales Manager, International Division of Minneapolis-Honeywell Regulator Company says:

> It is most desirable naturally for individuals we send abroad to have the ability to speak the language of the country to which they are being assigned. If there are two people both of equal technical background and one has the language ability, we would naturally hire the latter in preference to the one who did not have such an ability.
>
> Consequently, we feel that knowing a foreign language is a very important asset which can for any individual give him an opportunity which probably otherwise would not be open to him.

Trade with Latin America looms large in all United States export-import statistics. According to the Department of Commerce, for 1959 the total export of merchandise to 20 American republics amounted to $4.2 billion with an income value of $3.6 billion. Latin America was second only to Europe as a market for United States exports, taking 26 per cent of our commercial exports. A larger percentage of manufactured goods went to Latin America. One third or more of all exports of machinery, transportation equipment, iron and steel mill products, and pharmaceutical products went there. Mexico took the largest number of United States exports, with Venezuela, Cuba, and Brazil following in that order.

The 1959 report also states that Latin America was the principal source of our imports, 28 per cent of the total comprising over half of our purchases of foreign foods, and one fourth of industrial materials. Imports of oil play a major role. In fact, shipments of petroleum from Venezuela made up 84 per cent of its exports to the United States. Brazil's coffee ranked second, and Cuba's sugar ranked third.

In 1958 our trade with 20 American republics amounted to $4 billion in exports and $3.5 billion in imports. For Western Europe the corresponding figures were $4.4 billion and $3.2 billion.

It is obvious that in the export trade a knowledge of Spanish and Portuguese is valuable. H. F. Wiggs, Personnel Director, Ebasco International Corporation, states.

> . . . Our major need for young people to go to Latin America to participate in our operations is, first, for engineers—electrical, mechanical, and civil—and, second, for accountants . . . It is needless to say that those with a foreign language, especially Spanish or Portuguese, would fit better in their respective positions in Latin America.

A number of large export houses train their personnel themselves. This is done, for example, by W. R. Grace & Company, a concern which has dealt with South America for over a hundred years. In addition to the parent company in New York, there are 70 subsidiary and affiliated companies, employing approximately 20,000 persons in the United States and various foreign countries. The company is eager to secure qualified young people and publishes a booklet entitled *Op-*

portunities for Young Men in W. R. Grace & Co. (For various reasons, women are not sent abroad.) As to linguistic competence the personnel manager comments:

Inasmuch as our foreign dealings are primarily with Latin American countries a knowledge of the Spanish language is very valuable to our employees. The ability to speak the Spanish language is a basic consideration in assigning employees to our Latin American offices. The knowledge of this language is also useful in our New York office, inasmuch as we have a certain amount of correspondence in Spanish and have numerous occasions to speak with people from Latin American countries.

The preëminence of Spanish in export is also shown by its primacy in the commercial literature in that field. There are 96 United States publications whose principal circulation is in foreign countries; of these 48—that is, exactly half—are in Spanish. The amount of advertising in these magazines is increasing constantly. The Spanish edition of *Life* carries copy of over 80 American firms.

Banking is another field in which a knowledge of foreign languages is an asset. A number of our larger banks, such as the Chase Manhattan Bank and the First National City Bank, maintain branches abroad. Only a proportion, however, of the employees in foreign countries are Americans. On the other hand, there are excellent opportunities in the Translation Departments here.

This is true, too, of the foreign banks that have branches in the United States. Emilio Mayer, President of the Banca Commerciale Italiana, stresses the need for linguistically trained personnel:

Quite frequently we receive inquiries from banks or other firms engaged in foreign trade seeking office help with a knowledge of foreign languages. The inquiries pertain to receptionists, secretaries, male clerks, department heads, and officers, and the languages most in demand are Spanish, Italian, French, and German.

It has been my experience that the request greatly exceeds the supply, especially if a thorough knowledge of the language is required. It seems to me that the knowledge of a foreign language gives an immediate advantage to anyone seeking a job. Furthermore, the chances for advancement are far greater, not to mention the pleasant possibility of travel abroad.

An officer in the Personnel Department of the First National City Bank, the leading United States Bank in the International field, comments as follows:

. . . in our Translators Department. This unit is composed of some 38 translators who cover most of the commercial languages of the world. They handle all foreign correspondence, laws, contracts, governmental reports, financial and trade magazines, etc., in fact, practically every kind of foreign communication. The standard requirements are typing experience and ability to handle expertly at least two foreign languages. . . . These positions are held by both men and women. . . .

We have conducted overseas training projects since 1915. . . . When we have large enough classes we arrange for courses in conversational and banking Spanish or Portuguese. Otherwise the language training does not take place until the men land in Paris, Rio de Janeiro, Manila, Tokyo, Hong Kong, Singapore, Bombay, etc.

. . . Furthermore, our experience has taught us that it is more important to understand the customs, manners, and social mores of a foreign city than to understand just the language. Accordingly, we have established training centers, or "staging points" through which we feed our foreign recruits on their way to careers abroad. Therefore, when a man reaches his final assignment, he has had intensive training both in banking and in languages.

Officials in banks and export firms emphasize the importance of knowledge of a foreign language. Alex. J. Wertis, Personnel Manager of the United States Steel Export Company, says:

The ability to speak or to learn a foreign language is a tremendous asset. The greatest criticism of Americans in foreign lands in the past has been their reluctance to meet other peoples halfway about language. Other peoples take as much pride in their language and culture, as we do in ours. To address them in their own speech is a compliment to their language and culture. It gives you a headstart in personal relations. . . .

The extension of airlines to all parts of the globe has made the most distant peoples our neighbors. It makes communication with them in their own tongue imperative. In fact, all American airlines flying to foreign countries require at least part of their personnel to be able to speak a foreign language. George Gardner, Educational Director of Pan American Airways, says:

> As you know, Pan American World Airways routes go to all countries around the world. Employees who are sent to those other countries of course have to be able to speak the language of the country and this means that we have to have employees who speak Spanish, French, German, and Portuguese, and probably in some cases still other languages. Pilots generally are qualified in a foreign language and on a good many routes knowledge of a foreign language is required for stewards. In Latin America they have to be able to speak Spanish because many of their passengers speak no other language.

FOREIGN LANGUAGES—THE *SINE QUA NON* OF THE FOREIGN SERVICE

The United States is represented abroad by some 6,000 men and women in the Foreign Service. They are entrusted with the formal and official guarding of our interests in foreign countries.

Besides the Foreign Service officers, there are the official representatives of various Federal agencies, comprising about 100,000 persons. They are assigned to such bodies as the United States Information Agency, the International Co-operation Agency, the Department of Commerce, the Department of Agriculture, the Department of Labor and other agencies. Then there are the personnel of the Central Intelligence and the National Security Agencies. The largest number, however, are in the military: there are over a million American officers and men stationed all over the world.

The duties of Foreign Service officers, as defined in a Presidential order are:

1. To establish and maintain friendly relations between the Government and people of the United States and the government and people of the country to which they are accredited;
2. To keep the Government of the United States informed regarding political and economic developments abroad, particularly those affecting its interests;
3. To extend protection to American citizens and promote just American interests in every proper manner;
4. To interpret faithfully the viewpoint of the American government in any question at issue.

Now, these aims can be carried out effectively only with a knowledge of foreign languages. Unfortunately, until very recently, our foreign representatives have not been particularly well-equipped in that regard. In fact, a widespread lack of any competence in a foreign language has distinguished American diplomats.

It has been said that in 1946 the State Department did not have a single member on its staff in the Middle East who could read an Arabic newspaper. In order to know what was going on, our representatives had to mail the papers home to the Library of Congress for translation.

In 1949 the first American specifically trained for service in our embassy in Indonesia arrived. He discovered that a strong Communist-inspired anti-American sentiment was sweeping the country. The embassy had been totally unaware of this, for the native translators hired by the Americans had politely submitted only items favorable to the United States.

Since then conditions have improved, but even as late as January 25, 1954 an Under Secretary of State commented: "Our training in the Department has reached a sort of an all-time low . . . We found to our astonishment that we did not have one single officer or staff officer in the Czech Embassy who spoke Czech."

In the past many of our ambassadors and consuls have not

known the language of the country to which they were accredited and made no attempt to learn it. This would be unheard-of in the case of other nations. The former French ambassador to Germany not only spoke the language fluently but was also an authority on German literature.

Ignorance of the language on the part of our ambassadors has been almost the rule rather than the exception. Our first representative in Israel knew no Hebrew. Our recent ambassadors to Germany and Italy had to hurry to learn something of the respective language before assuming their assignments.

With the present urgency in international affairs, the importance, yea, the extreme urgency, of a knowledge of foreign languages on the part of our representatives abroad is apparent to the State Department. Competence in one foreign language was always theoretically required of a Foreign Service officer. The difficulty, however, of securing adequately trained personnel led to a relaxation of the qualifications. Even now a candidate for the position of Foreign Officer is given five years in which to make up the foreign language requirement.

Not until 1946 was a Foreign Service Institute established in the Department of State to prepare diplomats and to train some of them as language and area specialists. There is also a division of Language Services which does translations. However, as late as January, 1954 the Director of the Office of Personnel complained, "The present number of officers of the Foreign Service who have been given intensive full-time training in the language and areas pertinent to critical spots throughout the world is inadequate to meet the needs of the Service."

The lack of linguistic preparation has been a serious handicap to our representatives abroad. After investigating the Central Intelligence Agency, the Hoover Commission recommended the development of a "comprehensive, co-ordinated program" . . . "to expand linguistic training among American citizens serving the intelligence effort . . ."

Various suggestions have been made to create a reservoir of specialists in foreign languages. The United Nations offers a bonus to nonprofessional employees who learn another foreign language. It has also been recommended that the Federal government provide scholarships for especially able students of foreign languages, so that there may be a pool available whenever the need arises. President Caswell of Teachers College suggests the establishment of a national foundation for the encouragement and support of foreign language study.

Linguistic skill is needed in all our agencies which gather political, economic, military, and cultural information in various parts of the world. The same is true of the technical assistance programs.

The situation is an urgent one, especially when we see what the Soviet Union is doing. Their language program is an intensive and a long-range one. Not only are the familiar, well-known West European languages taught, but experts are trained in many of the less known languages of Asia and Africa. The Russians simply do not send anyone to a foreign country who does not know the language.

The picture presented by our own foreign representatives is pathetic by comparison. Howard E. Sollenberger, Dean of the School of Languages of the Foreign Service Institute, states:

> In a recent survey of our diplomatic service we found that 42.7 per cent of our diplomatic corps do not have a useful speaking and reading knowledge of any foreign language, and that 50 per cent do not have a useful speaking and reading knowledge of even such common languages as French, German, or Spanish. . . .

In order to obtain competent people, the Department of State spends much time and money training candidates in the Foreign Service Institute. The Department of Defense, too, maintains its own training centers like the Army Language School at Monterey, California, and the intensive language programs in some universities. Even more urgent is the need for competent linguists in the information and intelligence agencies. These agencies have finally come to the realization that they cannot function effectively without a knowledge of foreign languages.

At the end of World War II they still thought they could. A commission of American educators and experts was sent to Tokyo to reform the Japanese educational system; they had to work through interpreters. In Germany an elaborate system for democratizing and "re-educating" the Germans was set up. Twenty-five beautiful and well-equipped information centers, called "America Houses," were organized. Some 36 educational, technical and publicity bureaus, with tens of thousands of employees, elaborate offices, new housing, and a huge pool of motor cars were spread over Western Germany. But the one important factor needed to make this impressive machine effective was missing: very few of the officers and of those in charge could speak German fluently. In fact, they had to rely on their staff of German employees to implement the informational and educational program. Fortunately, the Germans, for various reasons, were helpful, co-operative, and loyal and so the program did achieve some results.

That this will no longer work is clearly evident. Hence, the United States Information Agency is looking for people who know not only German, or French and Spanish, but Russian and the less known languages. If our propaganda is to have any success, it must be conducted by competent linguists. Imagine the Voice of America without its staff of language experts!

Our official State Department radio station broadcasts in 37 foreign languages and English. Every day 88½ hours of broadcasting are sent to the four quarters of the globe. Programs are beamed to the Soviet Union in Russian, Ukrainian, Georgian, Armenian, Estonian, and Lithuanian. German radio stations are supplied with additional material which they can re-broadcast.

Strangely enough, comparatively little is done for Latin America. There is only one hour of Spanish daily. No program is provided in Portuguese.

The programs to Africa are done in Arabic, French, and English. None of the native African languages is used.

The State Department also issues magazines in foreign languages. One of the most attractive, in the format of *Life,* is the one in Russian entitled *Amerika.*

In fact, in all the various areas in which Americans are trying to influence or to help foreign peoples, knowledge of the language plays a decisive role. This is as true of technical assistance staffs as of intelligence agencies. It is not enough to hand out funds or to distribute machines; we must build up good will. That can only be done through language. That is the gateway to the intellectual and spiritual life of a people. Otherwise, we will have no close contact and no friendly relations.

This is the sad state of affairs which we are now facing all over the world. America has been generous, in fact, lavish with foreign aid, with technical assistance funds, with loans. But we have not made friends. We have lost China completely; we are hanging on to Taiwan and Korea. Large sections of Latin America are hostile to the United States. The Swedes are suspicious. Even little Iceland is annoyed with Americans. There are few areas in which Americans are hailed with enthusiasm.

Other countries have been far more successful, commercially and diplomatically. The British and the Germans are extending their influence and their trade throughout South America; the Russians and the Chinese are making headway in Asia. Their success is due in large measure to the careful preparation which they give their representatives in the culture, the psychology, and the language of the foreign people. The extent of that training and its success in the case of Soviet emissaries is described in *The Ugly American.*

Fortunately, our leaders have become aware of the urgency

of language training. The Department of State in August, 1957 issued circular No. 267 explaining its policy with reference to foreign languages in the Foreign Service. Every officer is to acquire a "useful" knowledge of two foreign languages within five years. The adjective "useful," as used here, means a sufficient competency so that the officer can read technical articles in one special field, and nontechnical news; that he can handle professional discussions in one or more special fields; and that he can use the spoken language in everyday situations. Time may be taken out for language lessons.

Specific directions are given as to the choice of a second language. The directive states:

1. When the officer's first-acquired foreign language is French, German, or Spanish, the second language selected may be one of these three in which the officer is not already proficient, or he may select Italian or Portuguese or one of the languages required by the Department in connection with area specialization, such as Arabic, Burmese, Chinese, Czech, Finnish, Greek, Hebrew, Hindi-Urdu, Hungarian, Indonesian, Japanese, Korean, Persian, Polish, Rumanian, Russian, Serbo-Croatian, Thai, Turkish, Vietnamese, etc.
2. When a language other than French, German, or Spanish is acquired first, one of these three languages normally will be the second language studied.

That this stress on foreign language preparation was necessary, is shown by the results of a survey made by the Department of State during 1956. This study of the language competence of 4,041 officers in the Foreign Service showed that less than half of the personnel possessed a useful proficiency in French, German, or Spanish. To overcome this deficiency the activities of the Foreign Service Institute in Washington have been extended. Full-time training is provided in French, German, and Spanish to about 500 students each year. There are 6 hours of classwork daily for 6 months in West European languages, and for 11 months in other languages. Classes are small; there are but a half dozen students. The instructor is a native speaker.

In order to make it possible for personnel stationed abroad to get the benefit of this training, branches have been established in Mexico, Nice, and Frankfort. In addition, classes in foreign languages are conducted under Institute supervision at 135 posts overseas.

This is all very encouraging. It is, however, deplorable that all this training has to be given to adults, already embarked on a career, and at considerable expense to the State Department, when it might have been provided in high school. The urgent need for linguistically trained personnel in the Foreign Service, in the intelligence agencies, and in the armed forces, is an additional motivation for the study of foreign languages in our schools and colleges.

FOREIGN MISSIONARIES NEED FOREIGN LANGUAGES

One vocation which, strange to say, has rarely been mentioned in connection with foreign language study is that of the foreign missionary. Here is a field of endeavor in which tens of thousands of persons of all nations are engaged, which covers the entire globe, and which embraces all languages. Indeed, it is an area which has been intimately linked to foreign language study ever since missionary endeavor began. Knowledge of the foreign language is indispensable to the missionary, for his aim is to change the religious thinking of communities speaking a foreign language. This situation has made it imperative for the missionary not only to acquire a speaking knowledge of the foreign tongue, but the ability to translate technical matter into an idiom which often lacks the very terminology needed.

In a number of instances it was the missionary who made the first serious study of the language and supplied it with a system of writing. Examples are Bishop Cyril who gave the Russians their Cyrillic alphabet, and Wulfilas, missionary to the Goths, who translated the Bible into their language and provided that language with its written form. The work of this missionary of the eighth century, preserved in Uppsala, Sweden, is the one great monument of Gothic which we possess. And in the early days of the Massachusetts Colony, John Eliot translated the New Testament for the converted Indians. It was the first printed book in the language of the aborigines; it was the first New Testament published in the New World.

In South America Spanish missionaries and priests, especially Dominicans, studied the Indian languages, composing grammars and devising a script. An example of this is Quechua, the language of the Incas, which is still spoken by untold thousands of Indians in the Andes Mountains.

This process is still going on. One of the noblest characters of this era, next to the missionary Schweitzer, is the missionary Laubach. It is he who has undertaken to solve the staggering problem of illiteracy in underdeveloped countries. He, too, has worked with alphabets and scripts in a dozen languages and has devised a method for the rapid learning of reading.

The missionary, again and again, throughout the centuries, has been the precursor of Western culture in distant lands. It is he who has laid the foundations for civilized life. This has been possible only because he has been in possession of the indispensable tool—competence in the foreign language.

Missionary activity is as great as ever. In fact, the number of American missionaries is on the increase. The total number of Americans representing Protestant denominations in foreign countries is 25,058. Catholic missionaries equal this number if they do not exceed it.

A tabulation of some of the leading missionary fields reveals the following:

Number of Missionaries Serving in Various Countries

PROTESTANT AND ROMAN CATHOLIC

(According to the *Bulletin of Missionary Research Library,* May, 1958)

	Protestant	*Roman Catholic*
Caribbean Area:		
Jamaica	407	173
Cuba	254	46
Haiti	523	28
Puerto Rico	120	568
Latin America:		
Argentina	700	11
Bolivia	522	108
Brazil	979	273
Chile	198	119
Colombia	279	33
Ecuador	208	123
Mexico	551	53
Nicaragua	65	45
Paraguay	113	15
Peru	447	113
Uruguay	79	2
Venezuela	317	23
Near East:		
Egypt	207	18
Iran	134	136
Lebanon	61	34
Israel	130	41
Algeria	112	
Morocco	86	1021
Africa:		
Belgian Congo	2146	3835
Ethiopia	344	16
French Equatorial Africa	534	376

	Protestant	Roman Catholic
Africa—(Continued)		
French West Africa	389	930
Ghana	238	232
Kenya	527	332
Liberia	327	33
Madagascar	112	726
Nigeria	1435	554
Southern Rhodesia	631	571
Northern Rhodesia	370	350
Sierra Leone	149	47
Tanganyika	672	1227
Uganda	73	690
Union of South Africa	820	426
Asia:		
Hong Kong	400	270
India	5656	3784
Indonesia	200	2206
Japan	2887	1176
Korea	298	162
Malaya	372	317
Pakistan	496	448
Philippines	774	453
Taiwan	353	106
U.S.S.R. (Asia)	483	161
New Guinea & Papua	564	264
New Hebrides	101	61

It is obvious, then, that American missionary endeavors are extensive and widespread. They cover the globe and reach almost every people. The missionary, like the foreign service officer and the businessman, represents America. He is engaged in building up friendly relations; in fact, it is his aim to spread good will. To do this effectively, however, he must be able to handle his medium of communication—the foreign language.

Because of the rapid extension of means of transportation, chiefly by air, the number of travelers has increased tremendously. Everyone is eager to go on a trip, even if it is only to Bermuda. Cruises are advertised in hyperbolic terms. The air lines proclaim the excellence of their cuisine, their free champagne, and the fact that you can pay for the trip on the installment plan.

Years ago it was the English who were the inveterate travelers. So overwhelming a proportion of tourists were from the British Isles that in some countries, like Spain, "English" and "traveler" were used synonymously. The English "discovered" and made accessible many a town which is today a standard tourist center. There are dozens of cities in Italy to which they drew attention. It was no less a person than Byron who put Venice at the top of the tourist's "musts," and he also named the Bridge of Sighs. In "Childe Harold" he sings:

> I stood in Venice on the Bridge of Sighs,
> A palace and a prison on each hand:
> I saw from out the wave her structures rise
> As from the stroke of the enchanter's wand.

One of Edward VII's favorite summer places was little Homburg in West Germany; so many aristocrats followed him there that on one occasion he remarked that there were undoubtedly more earls and dukes there than in London. It is in this picturesque spa that the hat originated which bears the name Homburg.

One might almost say that the French Riviera was a British discovery. Natives of the cold, blustery, northern island came to this warm delightful region around the middle of the eighteenth century. The English colony in Nice was so large that, at the suggestion of an Anglican clergyman, a broad boulevard along the shore was constructed for their convenience and named the *Promenade des Anglais*.

As in so many other areas, Americans have also become the leaders in travel. In 1959, over 7 million of our citizens went abroad. In the last 5 years applications for passports have increased by 50 per cent. The State Department has to provide 1½ million travelers with them. (Canada, Mexico, and some Latin-American countries do not require a passport.) Shortly before the season begins, the passport offices are crowded with applicants. It used to take six weeks to get the document; now it may be secured in three days. One day in 1959, the central office in Washington and the eight agencies issued 5,300 passports, or 11 a minute.

The volume of travel is so large that it makes a difference in international balances. According to Department of Commerce figures, Americans spend over $2,300,000,000 a year during their travels. Of course, this is rather one-sided; travel is an export for us. Only about half a million foreigners visit our shores, owing to the expense and the dollar exchange restrictions imposed by many countries.

The huge volume of American travel has other aspects, however, besides the economic. Each tourist is not merely a dispenser of cash but also a representative of his country. He brings with him good will or ill will. Within recent years the State Department has become so conscious of this fact that each prospective traveler receives, together with his passport, a booklet with a message from the President, urging him to be on his best behavior abroad. Unfortunately, in the past, some of our fellow countrymen have not deported themselves too well and the American tourist has acquired a reputation for impatience and ignorance. On the other hand, he has not been accused of being a tightwad and so his generous tips have usually assuaged hurt foreign feelings and have made him a welcome guest. But how much more enjoyable his stay in the foreign country would be and how much more could he do to build up friendly feelings toward America if he knew the language!

5 · "But, Does It Pay to Know a Foreign Language?"

YOUNG people planning a career often say, "Learning a foreign language is all right, but can I get a job with it?" The answer is definitely yes, especially if the applicant is proficient in some other technical skill.

With the present dominant position of the United States in world affairs there is an urgent demand for men and women who are in command of a foreign language. The need is evident in four major areas: the export business, various domestic vocations and professions, in the government service, and in teaching.

An inspection of the help wanted ads in any of our larger metropolitan daily newspapers will reveal an appreciable number and a great variety of interesting and remunerative positions. A study of the want ads of the Sunday edition of *The New York Times* resulted in a compilation of 608 jobs requiring foreign language competence. The languages represented, in order of frequency, were Spanish, French, German, Italian, and Portuguese, with 74 in various combinations. There were 359 requests for Spanish alone. The types of positions ranged from clerks at $50 a week to executives at $12,000. In fact, practically every Sunday there are over a hundred want ads in *The Times* asking for personnel with knowledge of a foreign language. Frequently combinations are requested: French-German, German-Spanish, French-Spanish, Portuguese-Spanish.

It is evident, then, that there are many interesting positions waiting for qualified persons with foreign language training together with technical skill. Knowledge of the foreign language alone will not, in most cases, secure the job, but it is an important, and in some cases, an essential asset.

One of the best portals of entry to an attractive business career is by way of a secretaryship. There is a wide demand for bilingual secretaries, especially in firms having international relations. Foreign departments are maintained by large business concerns, banks, and advertising agencies. These are staffed by personnel trained in one or a number of foreign languages. Usually the work is interesting; the salary is good. There are many opportunities for advancement from a secretaryship to a higher position.

Export houses have need of bilingual secretaries. Other positions are those of export assistant, assistant foreign credit manager, trade analyst, correspondent, consular invoice clerk, assistant traffic manager, and executive assistant. In connection with these positions the knowledge of a foreign language is frequently essential. The languages most in demand are Spanish, French, and Portuguese. In view of the constantly expanding foreign trade of the United States, there are excellent opportunities in the import-export field. Sometimes, too, there are opportunities for foreign travel.

Knowledge of a foreign language is useful not only in connection with correspondence but even more so for sales promotion and advertising. The latter is no longer limited to the printed page; the newest and most effective media are radio and television. The use of these means of communication is so important for the success of foreign trade, that the field of export advertising has been growing by leaps and bounds.

The *Directory of Foreign Publications* lists over 600 foreign newspapers and magazines that have representatives in the United States. Among the languages in which these publications appear are French, Spanish, Portuguese, German, Dutch, Italian, Norwegian, Swedish, Hebrew, Turkish, and Hindi.

There is also a list of almost one hundred American publications whose principal circulation is in foreign countries. These are primarily technical magazines concerned with a wide variety of products. Among them are automobiles, antibiotics, beverages, farm implements, office furniture, pharmaceutics, oil, textiles, tools, and chemicals. A considerable amount of advertising appears in the 30 international foreign language editions of *Reader's Digest.*

One large publishing house which gets out a number of technical magazines, maintains a staff of expert translators who are conversant with all fields of industry and engineering. An overseas staff is distributed in 75 different countries.

Printed advertising has expanded but the growth of radio and television advertising has been phenomenal. The Pan-American Broadcasting Company maintains a service which extends over 125 stations in most of the world's markets. The *Export Trade and Shipper* lists over 360 foreign radio and television stations and their United States representatives. The Latin-American countries are particularly well represented. For example, Brazil has 92 stations, Chile 19, Cuba 33, Mexico 19, and Venezuela 16.

Besides positions in world trade, in the Foreign Service, and in teaching, where a language is of prime importance, there are numerous activities in which a knowledge of a foreign language is useful and highly desirable. There are given aspects of certain lines of work in which linguistic proficiency is extremely helpful, as in the case of librarians, research workers, and radio announcers. The knowledge of a language or languages increases the efficiency of the employee and means more dollars in his pay envelope.

This is particularly true in professions where acquaintance with progress in the given field in other countries is necessary.

Dean Arnaud of the School of Architecture at Columbia University points out that "it is important for well-educated professionals . . . to at least have a reading knowledge of either French or German. . . . In the case of Columbia University, we require the entering students to have passed the intermediate language course in either French or German."

There are a limited number of openings for qualified linguists in the publishing field. There are about thirty publishers of foreign language books in this country who have small but highly reliable staffs of editors and proofreaders, as well as translators. In larger cities like New York there are also dealers in foreign books. One of the oldest of these, Stechert-Hafner, has 100 employees, most of whom know a foreign language or two.

One of the most interesting though limited fields for persons with a foreign language competence is journalism. There are local staffs of translators and foreign correspondents in different parts of the world. For such positions a high degree of expertness is required. L. B. Mickel of the United Press Association comments:

> The United Press application for employment asks: "What languages other than English do you speak and write *fluently?*" We are not interested in those who reply: "Had four years of German" or "Can read Spanish," etc. For instance, we expect a man on our Paris staff to be able to understand French from an excited native trying to send in a story on the phone. If you can handle news on the phone in a foreign language you have to be good. If a man says he can speak Russian we expect him to understand a Russian broadcast and be able to report it accurately. Since 58 countries throughout the world receive United Press news, it's safe to say we are interested in nearly all foreign languages."

And H. W. Burch of the United Press Association writes:

> Command of at least one foreign language long has been almost a necessity in the world press association field for any aspiring journalist, since so great a part of news gathering and distribution passes beyond local or national boundaries. The importance, there-

fore, of foreign language study for anyone hoping to enter world journalism is plain.

The expansion of world communications also has brought new emphasis to the need for foreign language study. This applies in many ways: the great increase in world travel has brought many more foreign students and journalists into contact with each other, forcing them to increase their language facility; a vast increase in the volume of news which can be delivered to remote points by modern radio channels has brought all public information media into closer, speedier contact; the pressures of hot and cold wars, and the dislocations accompanying them have forced interchanges between populations, and accompanying exchange of language habits; vast numbers of young U.S. men and women have worked, traveled and fought abroad as members of the U.S. Armed Forces or representatives of government agencies, greatly increasing their contact with foreign languages. . . .

As distribution of news abroad increases with the aid of new radio and telegraphic communications devices demand increases for editorial workers capable of handling one or more languages. The United Press now transmits its entire news report to Latin America in Spanish, with a full translation-editorial staff employed in New York solely for the purpose of writing the service in Spanish.

It also is worth noting that as the United States has assumed leadership in so many fields of world activity, New York and Washington have become the headquarters for many offices and directive bureaus employing translators, interviewers, commentators, and executives with a command of languages. The government itself, through its propaganda and diplomatic branches, is an extensive employer of persons equipped with more than one language. The United Nations headquarters in New York require many translators. . . .

There are, in fact, so many visible opportunities for the bilingual or trilingual person that no persuasion should be needed for the aspiring student or adult to perfect himself in a foreign language.

As pointed out by Mr. Burch, the vast increase in electronic devices and the rivalry in international relations has raised the area of communications to one of prime importance. With radio and television even the most distant and backward peoples may be reached.

For the radio announcer, even on local stations, the ability to speak, or at least read aloud, a foreign language or two is an asset. In fact, this ability is demanded of them every day, for they are called upon to announce the titles of operas and classical music selections, the names of foreign celebrities, geographical place names, and snatches or phrases in a foreign language.

Kenneth H. Baker, Director of Research of the National Association of Broadcasters, comments in *Vocational Opportunities for Foreign Language Students* as follows:

> . . . opportunity for the use of foreign languages in broadcasting would be in the actual reading of scripts in one of the many languages broadcast over standard American radio stations. A list of these languages includes: Italian, Polish, Spanish, Jewish, German, Czech, Slovak, Portuguese, Lithuanian, Hungarian, Scandinavian, Greek, French, Finnish, Yugoslavian, Ukrainian, Chinese, Russian, Japanese, Rumanian, Arabic, Dutch, Albanian, Syrian, Latin, Egyptian, Armenian.
>
> In addition to these languages, the short-wave broadcasts to other countries are also opportunities for the use of foreign languages. In this case, excellence of accent is especially desirable. . . .

International broadcasting is expanding continually. Arno G. Huth, Consultant to the Pan-American Broadcasting Company, writes in one of their *World Wide Special Reports:*

> Wartime and postwar developments have given international broadcasting great impetus, and have increased its scope and significance beyond all expectations. Today, international broadcasts, supplemented by the international exchange of television programs, originate in almost every country of the world and reach almost every nation. In the United States alone, no less than six agencies and organizations are engaged in international broadcasting. And like Great Britain and the Soviet Union, which operate the two most important international broadcasting services, Canada, Argentina, France, Italy, Poland, Czechoslovakia, Hungary, Indonesia, India, Pakistan, Australia, and many others are broadcasting day and night, and in many different languages.
>
> Even countries with a very limited number of radio sets have be-

come targets of international broadcasts. Arab listeners, owning fewer than 500,000 radio sets, may hear in addition nearly 250 hours per week of domestic Arabic broadcasts.

International broadcasting offers great potentialities for international advertising. There are, in various areas of the world, private as well as official stations which accept foreign-sponsored programs and which . . . are prepared to carry foreign-language programs destined to minority groups or to listeners in adjacent countries.

A high degree of technical facility is required of linguists in fields of scientific research. This type of work demands a thorough grounding in various sciences as well as in foreign languages. Especially since the beginning of our rivalry with the Soviet Union, the reading of scientific abstracts has assumed huge proportions. According to the director of the Engineering Societies Library in New York, some of the translating is done by a small and highly competent staff. Much of the material, however, is farmed out to specialists who know the language and the particular field of science. The material appears in German, French, Russian, Portuguese, Italian, Spanish, Japanese, Swedish, and Dutch.

As is evident, in some fields a reading knowledge is paramount; in others speaking fluency is required. The latter is true of employees in hotels. Some of the larger hotels, especially in New York, maintain foreign departments. Languages required are French, Spanish, Portuguese, and German. The personnel director of the Waldorf-Astoria says that the head of their foreign department speaks 8 languages. Even a number of typists and stenographers are bilingual. He comments: "I think that the knowledge of a foreign language, or several languages, is an aid in securing employment in any large hotel where they would likely have a clientele from abroad. . . ." The managers of other large hotels express similar thoughts.

Knowledge of a foreign language is also important for librarians, especially in metropolitan areas, where the larger libraries have foreign book collections. Such knowledge is particularly useful in departments of science and technology.

German and French are the important languages, and more recently, Russian.

The New York Public Library has a number of departments in its central reference collection in which personnel with competence in foreign languages is employed. Many branch libraries maintain collections of foreign books. The 22 languages represented are Chinese, Croatian, Czech, Danish, Dutch, Finnish, French (9 branch libraries), German (8), Greek, Hebrew (3), Hungarian (3), Italian (5), Lithuanian, Norwegian, Polish, Portuguese, Russian, Slovak, Spanish (4), Swedish, Ukrainian, Yiddish (4).

The circulation department of the main library employs a number of assistants to aid foreign-born readers. The languages represented are French, German, Spanish, Italian, Russian, Czech, Polish, Hebrew, and Yiddish.

Of the 33 accredited library schools in the United States, 19 require a reading knowledge of one foreign language. Two schools require two languages. French and German are preferred.

A knowledge of foreign languages is especially needed in the American library service abroad, which was begun in 1946. These are the information libraries maintained in many foreign countries by the Department of State. The librarians need linguistic skill not only in their daily work but also because they are frequently called upon to attend international conferences. To show the extent of this project it may be pointed out that in 1951 there were 130 reading rooms and 25 information centers in West Germany alone.

In the metropolitan areas personnel with foreign language competence is found in most of the larger department stores. One such emporium in Brooklyn, New York, namely Abraham and Strauss, has some 300 employees who speak one or more foreign languages. There is a range of 29 languages. There are 85 speakers of Italian and fifty of German. Even less common languages are represented, as Latvian, Swedish, Norwegian, Japanese, Chinese, Syrian, Greek, Dutch, Danish, Finnish, Armenian, Hungarian, Turkish, Czech, Estonian, Polish, and Portuguese.

The demand for bilingual stenographers and secretaries is great. A survey of the want ad columns of the Sunday edition of the *New York Times* usually reveals from 60 to 75 jobs. On a given Sunday, for example, the following languages were asked for in connection with stenographers and secretaries: Spanish, 35; French, 9; Italian, 5; German, 3; French-Spanish, 3; French-German, 1; and one each for Dutch, Hebrew, and Yiddish. The degree of competence required was: able to take dictation, 5; "helpful," 5; knowledge of, 4; able to translate, 4; able to speak, 1; able to speak fluently, 1. The foreign language ability usually adds from $5 to $10 to the weekly salary.

There is a considerable demand for translators in business, in research organizations, and in the government service. In the New York classified telephone directory over 60 translation bureaus are listed. It is not easy work: the translator must be prepared to deal with commercial, legal, cultural, and technical material. The compensation is not generally very high. (More information is given about the position of translator in Federal offices on the following pages.)

Vocational opportunities in foreign languages are increasing continually. Professor Lois S. Gaudin of Brooklyn College made a survey of the want ads of six Sunday editions of the *New York Times* and summarized the results in "Careers in Modern Languages" (*Modern Language Journal,* May, 1960). A comparison of the number of jobs advertised in 1950–51 and 1959–60 revealed that there were 379 more positions in the United States, an increase of 62 per cent. The chief languages asked for were Spanish, 440; French, 147; German, 108; and Italian, 38. There were 175 combinations of languages. Salaries went as high as $13,000 for engineers and managers. One was for a $20,000 job. According to language and by percentages, the increase in the number of jobs for 1959–60 was: French 128 per cent, German 162 per cent and Spanish 23 per cent. The 1959–60 survey included 59 positions overseas—all for men. It is significant that the number of ads for teachers has tripled.

Aside from the many opportunities in the business world, there are a considerable number of interesting positions in government service which require knowledge of a foreign language. The largest number of Federal employees occupying such positions are translators and bilingual stenographers.

According to bulletins issued by the United States Civil Service Commission, "examinations for translator and bilingual stenographer positions test knowledge of, and aptitude in the use of, foreign languages." "Translators prepare written translations either from a foreign language into English, or from English into a foreign language. Some positions require translation of scientific material." "Bilingual stenographers perform work similar to that of other stenographers, except that they take and transcribe their notes in more than one language." "There are other federal positions in which a knowledge of one or more foreign languages is required or considered advantageous." "Examples would be a few specific positions, such as patrol inspector trainee (Immigration and Naturalization Service), scientific or engineering document analyst, specialist in foreign agriculture, research engineer, economist, physicist and chemist."

The most attractive positions in the Federal government that require knowledge of a foreign language are in the United States Foreign Service. It is a job for any young person who is eager to travel, who seeks adventure, and who has a strong desire to serve his country abroad.

Charles W. Curtis, Chief of the Recruitment Operations Branch, Division of Personnel, Department of State, comments:

In the Department of State, there are a number of types of positions which require foreign language facility in varying degrees. A high degree of language proficiency is a basic requirement for such positions as Information Officer, Cultural Affairs Officer, and Public Affairs Officer in the information program in Europe and Latin America.

. . . Our Division of Language Service employs Language Typists, Translators, Reviewers, and Interpreters . . . Most of the people occupying the positions now have had extensive foreign residence in addition to a thorough academic training. A minimum of two languages is necessary and the majority of these employees handle four or more . . . In the Interpreter-Reviewer-Translator category, we mainly use French, Spanish, Portuguese, and some German, Italian and Russian . . .

One of the most interesting fields of government service, especially for those eager to participate in international affairs, is the United States Foreign Service. This is the ideal branch for the career man. The basic requirements are: age, at least 20 but under 31 years; American citizen; if married, wife must be an American citizen.

The Foreign Service Officer keeps his government informed of the multitudinous developments abroad. He protects American citizens and American interests in foreign countries. He cultivates and maintains friendly relations with peoples of other nations. He negotiates treaties, conventions and protocols regarding international trade, tariffs, shipping, commerce, and the preservation of peace . . .

In other words, the work is unusually interesting. It is a position of responsibility and dignity. It is well remunerated.

There is an oral test, a physical test, and a series of 8 written examinations lasting 3½ days. Of these, 3 are called "special examinations"; the last one is in modern languages. It is 1½ hours or 3 hours in length. It tests ability to read with comprehension French, German, Portuguese, Russian, or Spanish. (No other languages are dealt with in the written examination. Each candidate is required to take only one of the languages but may offer two.) Officers failing to meet the language requirements within two years will be separated from the Service. In other words, passing the language examination is an indispensable qualification for the position.

There are about 20,000 United States diplomatic employees. Some 300 missions are stationed in 75 foreign countries. Almost 200,000 American civilians are employed in Federal agencies abroad. In addition, there are about 1,500 American technicians working on Point Four Projects in 35 countries.

A Civil Service bulletin announcing an examination for Translator lists the following languages:

Group I:

1. French	3. Italian	5. Spanish
2. German	4. Portuguese	

Group II:

1. Chinese	6. Hebrew	11. Rumanian
2. Czech	7. Hungarian	12. Russian
3. Danish	8. Japanese	13. Swedish
4. Dutch	9. Norwegian	14. Turkish
5. Greek (Modern)	10. Polish	15. Yiddish

16. Miscellaneous languages (other than those listed)

Applicants may apply for not more than six of the languages listed, except that no limit is placed on the number of languages for which application may be made under Miscellaneous Languages.

The written tests include:

1. A general qualifying test of verbal abilities (vocabulary, English usage, and paragraph reading) in English.
2. All competitors will take a translating test requiring a general knowledge of the language. In addition, they will take a test involving translation of selected material from the language into English, or selected material from English into the language, or both, at their choice.

Application forms for the examination may be obtained from any first class or second class post office, except in cities where a United States Civil Service regional office is located. These are as follows:

First Region: Post Office and Courthouse Building, Boston 9, Mass.

Second Region: Federal Building, Christopher Street, New York 14, N.Y.

Third Region: Custom House, Second and Chestnut Streets, Philadelphia 6, Pa.

Fourth Region: Third and Jefferson Drive SW, Tempo R, Washington 25, D.C.

Fifth Region: New Post Office Building, Atlanta 3, Ga.

Sixth Region: Post Office and Courthouse Building, Cincinnati 2, Ohio.

Seventh Region: New Post Office Building, Chicago 7, Ill.

Eighth Region: Post Office and Custom House Building, St. Paul 1, Minn.

Ninth Region: New Federal Building, St. Louis 1, Mo.

Tenth Region: Federal Office Building, 610 South Street, New Orleans 12, La.

Eleventh Region: Room 302, Federal Office Building, Seattle 4, Wash.

Twelfth Region: 129 Appraisers Building, San Francisco 11, Calif. Branch Offices: 514 Post Office and Courthouse Building, Los Angeles 12, Calif.; Federal Building, Honolulu 2, Hawaii.

There are, of course, many other types of jobs on lower levels with less exacting examinations and responsibilities. The State Department issues a booklet, *Opportunities for Employment Overseas,* which gives much valuable information regarding opportunities in the service. Aside from the top-level positions such as Chiefs of Missions, Foreign Service Officers, and Staff Officers, there are the following openings: secretary, stenographer, typist, clerk, diplomatic courier, radio operator, nurse, international information administrator, etc.

Under the list of qualifications appears this statement: "In addition to the usual clerical aptitude test, applicants must pass a language examination."

The Chief of the Recruitment Service says: "Recent college graduates interested in the Service are encouraged to take the Foreign Service Officer Examination which is scheduled annually in the fall. Candidates must offer one of the following languages: French, German, Russian, Spanish, and Portuguese."

The Technical Co-operation Administration in its leaflet entitled *Training for Point Four Careers* says: "Study at least one foreign language. Knowledge of one of the less common languages—Arabic, for example—may open the door to a job. It is a valuable asset when experience is limited."

There are approximately 1,500 American technicians working on Point Four Projects in 35 countries.

Another interesting field for linguists is the Voice of America. Broadcasting over a world network of 75 stations in 46 languages, it reaches possibly 3 million listeners. About 2,000 persons are employed by VOA. For so-called monitoring, foreign-born specialists are used—largely because native Americans with sufficient language competence have not been available.

Another beehive of foreign language activities is the office of the United Nations. There is a wide range of positions from bilingual typist to rapid-fire interpreters.

"The language posts of the United Nations Secretariat consist of translation, interpretation, verbatim reporting, summary reporting, proofreading, clerical and secretarial. English, French, Russian, Spanish, and Chinese are the official languages of the organization, and out of these English and French are considered as working languages: hence, staff may be needed to work in the capacities enumerated above in one or more of the specified languages."

"Openings for linguists are of two main sorts: on the one hand for bilingual secretaries and typists (English plus French or Spanish) and on the other for translators and interpreters. There are also occasional vacancies for Russian typists."

Examinations are held each year. A list of qualified candidates is compiled for appointments during the next fiscal year.

And finally, in connection with the consideration of positions in the Federal service, there are the armed forces. With the extension of our military to all corners of the globe, the need for a knowledge of foreign languages on the part of officers and men becomes almost imperative. Courses have been set up, especially in Paris, for the officers of NATO. More than half of the 2,000 officers and men at headquarters are enrolled.

The problem of equipping the armed forces with competence in languages is an extensive one, for there are over 1,000,000 military personnel and over 75,000 civilian employees stationed in almost 40 countries.

FOREIGN LANGUAGE TEACHERS ARE NEEDED

For the college graduate who has majored in a foreign language and who has literary and scholastic inclinations, teaching is a most attractive career. In the past the profession has suffered because of insufficient remuneration, but times have changed. The widespread public interest in languages and the generous financial and moral support of the Federal government have given a great impetus to the teaching of foreign languages. The demand for well-trained teachers is definitely on the increase.

This is pointed out in the State Department Discussion Guide, *The National Interest and Foreign Languages,* as follows:

> We lack accurate figures on the number of students of foreign languages among the 2¼ million persons now enrolled in our various colleges and universities. At a guess there are about 450,000. Assuming that this proportion does not change, and assuming the accuracy of predictions that total college enrollments will reach 3 millions by 1957–58, 4 millions by 1956–66, it would seem that a considerable number of additional language teachers need to be trained at once.

The foreign languages most widely taught in the public high schools of the United States are French, German, Latin, and Spanish. Until recently, Latin was numerically in the lead; at present Spanish is at the top. In addition to these 4 languages, there are certain areas and cities in which Italian, Hebrew, Polish, Norwegian, Portuguese, and Russian are taught. The colleges include a number of other European languages such as Hungarian, Dutch, Danish, and Czech. Larger universities maintain departments in which Oriental and African languages are studied. The Institute of Languages and Linguistics in Washington offers courses in Germanic, Romanic, Slavic, Semitic, and Far Eastern languages.

Approximately 1½ million students in the public high schools study a foreign language. In addition to this, there are possibly a half million foreign language students in private schools.

The FLES movement described previously is gaining momentum. Estimates are that some 600,000 pupils in grade schools are learning a foreign language. The languages taught are chiefly, French, Spanish, and German, with much smaller enrollments in Italian, Russian, Polish, and Portuguese. In view of the lack of teachers, many colleges have set up courses to train language teachers for the elementary schools.

The prospects, then, in the field of teaching are bright. It seems quite likely that language courses will be extended and that most public schools will be compelled to introduce at least one modern language. The trend among colleges is to increase the language requirement for admission.

All this points in the direction of a considerable increase in the demand for teachers. There are good jobs now; there will be many more in the future.

6 · The Babel of Tongues

IN WESTERN EUROPE

THE question has often been asked: Why do men speak so many tongues? Why don't we have one universal language? According to the Bible, men had a common tongue in the beginning, but by divine command the linguistic divisions arose. The Lord himself is responsible for the confusion of tongues, according to the account in Genesis. "And the whole earth was of one language, and of one speech." But when men began to build a tower which was to reach heaven, the Lord said, "Behold, the people is one and they have all one language . . . Go to, let us go down, and there confound their language, that they may not understand one another's speech." And so the building of the tower of Babel came to a standstill and men began to speak in different tongues.

Scientists are not agreed as to whether all languages had a common origin. The facts are that some languages are similar to one another; that others are so strange that they cannot be classified; that in the past languages have developed, lived, and died; that at present there are almost 3,000 languages in use. This plethora of tongues need not disturb us too much. There are only a dozen languages that have more than 60 million speakers. Hundreds of minor languages are spoken by small groups of African Negroes and by American Indians. Of the 12 languages with the largest number of speakers, 6 are European and 6 are Asiatic.

Let us skip around the world as on a magic carpet and listen to some of the languages spoken in different countries. If we should actually take an airplane to Europe, our first stop is likely to be Shannon in Ireland. While waiting in the airport our eyes catch the strange inscriptions, obviously meaning "entrance, exit, men, women, etc." They are in Irish, the newly revived national language which has been in general use only since the establishment of the Irish Republic.

The script is different from our Latin alphabet; it is derived from the writing of the monks of the Middle Ages and is thought to have been introduced by St. Patrick. Irish was spoken by a dwindling minority in the rural areas of the western part of the island when it was restored by official decree. Despite the enthusiasm of scholars and poets, and the pressure of the government, which requires the language as part of all civil service examinations, less than one fourth of the 3,000,000 inhabitants of Eire can speak Irish.

The tendency to re-establish an ancient native tongue as an official language is found all over the world where new nations have arisen. It is evident in Israel and India, in Iceland and Ceylon. All of the recently liberated African colonies are pursuing the same course. One may question the wisdom of crowding out world languages like English and French and trying to replace them by languages which are lacking in modern technical vocabulary, languages difficult to learn which are spoken by a comparatively small number of people. By adopting its own tongue a smaller people actually isolates itself from the broader streams of world culture and world communication. But human beings are motivated by emotion and sentiment rather than reason. Language is the chief cultural heritage of a people, to whom it is very precious; it is, therefore, a matter of national pride to preserve it.

It seems that the Celts once occupied most of Western Europe, living in a territory that extended from the Danube to the British Isles. Celts once dwelt in the valley of the Po, and the Italian dialect of that region still reveals some words of Celtic origin. However, invasions by Slavic and Germanic tribes drove them to the western edge of Europe, so that their descendants now live largely in Brittany, Wales, and Ireland.

In each of these regions a distinct language is spoken. In fact, there are two groups, the Goidelic or Gaelic, comprising Irish, Manx, and Scots Gaelic, and the Brythonic, or Cymric, comprising Breton, Cornish, and Welsh. Breton is spoken by about a million people, Welsh by approximately 3,000,000. Scottish Gaelic, the language of the highlands of Scotland and of the Hebrides, has probably no more than 100,000 speakers. There are also a few in Canada. Manx, spoken on the Isle of Man, is spoken by only ten people and Cornish, the native tongue of Cornwall, has passed away altogether. Irish is the national language of Eire but most of its natives speak English and not Gaedhilg, as it is officially known.

The Celtic languages are quite difficult because of complicated rules of pronunciation, in addition to archaic spelling, especially in Irish. In this language few words are pronounced as they are written. Changes in the forms of nouns and adjectives are another difficulty; they take place at the beginning and not at the end of the word. This change in sound and spelling is called "mutation" in the Gaelic group and "eclipsis" or "lenation" in the Cymric group. Furthermore, in Irish some changes also take place at the end of nouns. Like Scottish Gaelic, it has four cases. Breton and Welsh have practically only one case. Breton tends to stress the final syllable of a word; the other Celtic languages prefer next to the last syllable.

The Celtic languages are printed in Roman type except for Irish, which employs the so-called "Irish hand" used by the monks of the Middle Ages. Realizing that this is an added difficulty, there is now a movement on foot to substitute

Roman type; this, in fact, is being done in the case of some new books.

With much patriotic fervor the Irish have revived their ancient tongue and have made it a national language. The Welsh are equally proud of their Celtic speech. Both languages are faced with the problem that confronts all newly restored languages, e.g., Hebrew, of evolving words and expressions for thousands of modern concepts and situations. Instead of taking over words that have become international, the tendency is to form new words, generally compounds, out of native roots. This is a widespread linguistic phenomenon; it occurs in such diverse languages as German and Chinese.

Despite their differences, the various Celtic tongues are closely related. For example,

English	*Irish*	*Breton*	*Welsh*
arm	brac	breac'h	braich
friend	cara	kar	car
large	mor	meur	mawr
one	aon	un	un
three	tri	tri	tri
hundred	cead	kant	cant

Despite the tenacity with which the Celts cling to their ancient tongues, English is, of course, spoken by everyone throughout the British Isles. Here and there there are marked dialectic variations. This is evident in London where the native Cockney is sometimes quite unintelligible to the American tourist.

The pronunciation of certain English proper names startles the visitor. He is accustomed to "Wooster" for "Worcester" and "Gloster" for "Gloucester" but is nonplused when he hears Cholmondeley pronounced "Chumly," Magdalen College referred to as "Maudlin" College, and St. John called "Sinjun." There are differences, too, in vocabulary which amuse our fellow countrymen, like the following:

American	*British*
suspenders	braces
druggist	chemist
subway	underground
gas	petrol
truck	lorry
dessert	sweet

To these may be added a number of differences in pronunciation like clark for clerk, shedule for schedule, leftenant for lieutenant.

However, the differences are not too great. As Shaw expressed it facetiously, "England and America are two countries separated by the same language." The greatest number of speakers of English are outside of England, for what was originally the language of a people inhabiting a small island has become the world's most widely used medium of communication. For this English is especially well suited because of the simplicity of its structure, the absence of inflected forms, and the fact that it has borrowed from practically every language on the globe. Its vocabulary is the richest linguistic treasure house, for it contains words and concepts from all the important languages.

Now let us fly on to picturesque Amsterdam. There we hear the deep guttural sounds of a language which seems similar to English, especially when we see it in print. Some common words are spelled identically: water, warm, hand, ham, bank, hen, machine, pen, school, etc. Dutch, the language of 10 million Hollanders is closely related to English. So is Flemish, which is spoken by about half the Belgians. The other language of Belgium is French.

In connection with Dutch we come upon another linguistic peculiarity which exists in some countries, namely, a considerable difference between the spoken and the written language. Literary Dutch is, like German, highly inflected. It has three genders, four cases, adjective endings, strong and weak verbs. In everyday speech, however, the inflections and the case forms are generally discarded. For example, instead of employing the genitive *des vaders,* the preposition is used as in English, *van de vader* (of the father). The distinction between masculine and feminine nouns is dropped and the article for both becomes *de.* This simplifying tendency has gone farthest in the case of Afrikaans, the variety of Dutch spoken by the descendants of the settlers of South Africa.

As we cross the border into Germany we hardly notice the difference. The architecture is the same, the landscape does not change, and the language sounds identical. The fact is that Low German (Plattdeutsch), the dialect spoken throughout Northern Germany, is very close to Dutch.

And here we come upon a linguistic situation which prevails in many countries of Europe, namely, bilingualism. Everyone really speaks two languages. In northern Germany the average person uses Low German in the home, on the street, and in the daily affairs of life. However, in school, in the office, and in all official acts High German is the standard.

For a long time there was a struggle between Low German and High German, but finally the language of the high *(hoch)* regions, i.e., Central Germany, won. The language was primarily established through Luther's translation of the Bible, completed in 1537. Although the North Germans officially accepted Hochdeutsch, they have clung for sentimental reasons to their Plattdeutsch.

In other parts of Germany there are dialects which differ from the standard. This is particularly true of South Germany and Bavaria. A noticeable difference between the speech of the North and the South is the pronunciation of the *r.* In the North the uvular *r* is used, in the South the trilled *r* is current. In the North the tendency is to pronounce initial *sp* and *st* as in English; for example, *Spiel, Stein, Stock.* The South German uses the *sch*-sound not only initially, where it is standard, but also finally, saying *Poscht* for *Post, erscht* for *erst* and *ischt* for *ist.* Also the final *g* is always a *k* sound in the South, whereas in the North many Germans pronounce it like the *ch,* especially in the suffix *-ig* (N. G. *Könich,* S. G. *Könik,* "king").

German is spoken by a hundred million people. It is the language not only of Germany, but also of Austria, the western two thirds of Switzerland, Alsace in France, and the little principality of Luxemburg.

In Switzerland we again encounter a disparity between the literary language and the spoken tongue. The colloquial speech is so different from Hochdeutsch that it is called "Schwyzer-Dütsch."

German is the language of Zurich, Interlaken, and Lucerne. As we move west and enter Geneva and Lausanne, we are in French-speaking Switzerland.

But before continuing through Central Europe, let us fly up north to Oslo, the capital of Norway. The tongue we hear there, Norwegian, is in a state of linguistic flux. For four centuries Norway was under Danish occupation and its native tongue was practically crowded out. In fact, the two languages mingled to such an extent that they were known as Dano-Norwegian until recently. When Norway secured its independence in 1814, patriots like the poet Henrik Wergeland determined that the country was to have its own language. Although written Danish was retained, so many Norwegian elements were added that it became a different tongue. It is the language used by Björnson and Ibsen, and is the medium of expression for commerce, science, journalism, and the school. It is called *riksmal* or *bokmal.*

It is predominantly the speech of the cities. In the rural areas people continue to speak dialects derived from the Norwegian of ancient times. Purists and patriots have tried to restore the language to its original character. They have succeeded so well that there are now practically two languages in Norway, both officially recognized. The Norwegian of the rural areas is known as *landsmal* or *nynorsk* ("New Norsk").

Actually, Danes and Norwegians have little difficulty in understanding one another. This is fortunate, for tens of thousands of Norwegians—and Swedes, too—seek recreation and pleasure in Copenhagen, the largest Scandinavian city, which is lovingly referred to as "the Paris of the North."

Denmark once owned Iceland, which secured its independence in 1918 and complete autonomy in 1944, when it set up a republic. It is probably the oldest democracy in the world; in 1930 it celebrated the thousandth anniversary of its *Althing* or parliamentary assembly. It is the land of the ancient Eddas and Sagas and even the long occupation by the Danes made no impression on its culture and traditions. Its language is practically that of the Vikings and it retains the full panoply of its archaic inflections. It declines not only its nouns in four cases, but also the suffixed article. In conjugating verbs, a full set of endings is used.

The other Scandinavian languages have followed the tendency of other European tongues to drop cumbersome inflections and to simplify their structure. Every so often, for example, Danish spelling is modified, so as to make the written form more phonetic. This is done in a very sensible and painless manner. The Ministry of Education merely decrees that beginning with a certain date a given number of words will be spelled differently. It devolves upon the schools to teach the new spelling to the pupils. Within six months the order has been carried out and everyone is happy.

A distinctive feature of the Scandinavian tongues is the placing of the definite article after the noun. For example: *stol,* "chair," *stolen,* "the chair"; *barn,* "child," *barnet* "the child."

A curious difference between Norwegian and Swedish occurs in the pronunciation of *sk* so that one "skees" in Norway but "shees" in Sweden. Besides *ski,* the other universally known Scandinavian words are *skol* and *smorgasbord* (*smorrebrod* in Danish).

The Scandinavian languages are all pretty close to one another. In fact, they are also related to English, Dutch, and German. This can be seen by looking at the following words:

English	*Dutch*	*German*	*Danish*	*Nor-wegian*	*Swedish*	*Ice-landic*
father	vader	Vater	fader	far	fader	fadir
mother	moeder	Mutter	moder	mor	moder	modir
night	nacht	Nacht	nat	natt	natt	nott
good	goed	gut	god	god	god	godur
foot	voet	Fuss	fod	fot	fot	fotur

Because of their close relationship—which is due to a common origin—these languages are classified as belonging to the Germanic family. This linguistic category is in turn subdivided into the West Germanic branch and the North Germanic branch. The former includes English, Dutch, Flemish, and German; the latter is made up of the Scandinavian languages.

Now let us enter *la belle France*. Its language was established long ago by Paris and the surrounding region known as the *Île de France*.

French is spoken not only by 40 million natives of France but all over the world, especially in North Africa and in the former French colonial possessions. Although it is no longer exclusively the language of diplomacy—having been largely replaced by English—French enjoys prestige as the language of culture and refinement. During the seventeenth and eighteenth centuries when French influence was dominant in Europe, it was the language of all cultured people from Nantes to Nizhni-Novgorod. The extremely Prussian Frederick the Great disdained his native German and spoke and wrote French. The Russian aristocrats used that language so completely that at the time of Napoleon's invasion, when, for patriotic reasons, they tried to drop it, they found it difficult to speak their mother tongue correctly. Thousands of French words and expressions went over into other languages.

As in all European countries, however, there are dialects and even different languages in France. As we go west from Paris we enter Brittany where the natives speak Breton, a tongue entirely unrelated to French. As its name indicates, it comes from Britain; it is a Celtic language. As early as the fifth century, natives of Cornwall in southwest England began crossing the Channel and settling in what was then known as Armorica. Probably the invasion of England by the Saxons had driven them out. At any rate, so many of them came that gradually Armorica became Brittany. To this day the southwestern part is known as Cornouaille, that is, Cornwall. All of the older Bretons speak the ancient tongue; some disclaim any knowledge of French. It is interesting to note that although comparatively few Celtic words have entered French, the form of the word "eighty"—*quatre-vingts* ("four twenties") is of Breton origin.

In the south of France, in Provence, there is another tongue which sounds strange, namely, Provençal. It is, however, related to French. It was the language of the troubadours and has a rich literature. A number of poets and scholars have promoted Provençal with great zeal. Outstanding was the poet Fréderic Mistral, who, when offered membership in the French Academy, declined with the remark, "Why should I join a society that does not even speak French?" The implication, of course, was that Provençal was the real language of France. In the past there was considerable rivalry between the French of the north, known as *langue d'oui* and that of the south called *langue d'oc* (after the words for "yes"). Finally, the northern speech won and the language of the Île de France and of Paris became the standard.

Going farther west along the Pyrenees one of the strangest languages is encountered. Study and research have failed to identify this tongue, spoken by a million Basques, half of them in France and half in Spain. Basque has no relationship to French or Spanish; it is not even considered a European tongue, although some scholars think it is derived from the language of the original inhabitants of the Iberian peninsula. It is so difficult that according to one legend the devil was able to learn only one word of it after seven years of study.

Now let us fly on to Madrid, the capital of Spain. Many of

us had Spanish in school, so this language is not completely strange to us. In number of speakers it ranks fifth among the world's languages. It is not only the language of 30 million Spaniards but of 85 million Latin Americans. As in the case of French, the idiom of the capital and of the king became the national language. Castilian reduced the other varieties of Spanish to dialects such as Austrian, Galician, Valencian, Aragonese, etc.

In Barcelona, in northeastern Spain, we hear another tongue, Catalan, which is somewhat different from standard Spanish. The Catalonians, who are efficient and progressive—they like to be called "the Anglo-Saxons of Spain"—refuse to give up their language. In fact, at times they have demanded political autonomy.

Galician, spoken in the northwest, is closely related to Portuguese. The latter is the tongue of 9 million natives of Portugal. It is spoken in many parts of the world because of the intrepidity of the Portuguese as explorers. It was, after all, a Portuguese who first circumnavigated the globe. As in the case of a number of European countries, Portugal has more speakers of its language outside its boundaries than within. Portuguese is the language of Brazil, a country as large as the United States and with over 63 million inhabitants.

Americans, who are prone to simplify, like to assume that Spanish and Portuguese are pretty much the same. They think that Portuguese is merely a dialect of Spanish. In print the two often look similar. Actually, there are marked differences in pronunciation, spelling, grammar, and vocabulary. Portuguese has a wider variety of vowel sounds, including nasals, which are entirely absent in Spanish. The rules for the position of the object pronouns are quite different. There are hundreds of words which are written alike in both languages but which differ in meaning.

Now let us fly from Barcelona to Nice, and then to Rome. The language we hear spoken around us sounds somewhat like Spanish. The spelling is quite phonetic and the vowel sounds are clear and rich. This has made Italian the ideal language for singing. It differs from Spanish in its fondness for double consonants and in the absence of an accent mark for stress.

As the visitor wanders about the Eternal City he encounters everywhere ruins of ancient Rome—the baths of Caracalla, the Colosseum, the Forum, etc. The Romans left their mark on the architecture not only of the capital but of all of Italy.

They also left their mark on the language. Italian is extremely close to Latin; one might think of it as the modernized speech of the Romans. In his *Story of Language* Mario Pei stresses this close relationship between the two languages by citing a poem of eleven lines, written by an Italian high school student, which is identical, word for word, in Latin and in Italian.

As in other countries, the national language developed out of the speech of the people. The vernacular was looked down upon until it was employed as a literary vehicle by Dante, Petrarch, and Boccaccio. They chose the speech of Tuscany and thus it became the standard Italian. The various regional dialects, however, persist to this day. In fact, there are so many of them that they form groups, like those of Liguria, of Venice, of Naples, of Calabria, and of Sicily. Some of these, like Sicilian and Corsican, are so different from literary Italian that they are practically distinct languages. But they are all, like Tuscan Italian, descendants of Latin. So are French, Spanish, Portuguese, and Rumanian. For this reason they are classified as the Romance family of languages. About 300 million people speak the languages of this group which is, after the Germanic, the second largest linguistic category of Europe.

Latin first appeared about 500 B.C. as the language of a small tribe settled near the mouth of the Tiber. Around them were other tribes, some speaking related languages like Oscan and Umbrian, others like the Etruscans using an unrelated tongue. In the valley of the Po there were Gauls who spoke Celtic and in Sicily there were Greeks. On the latter island there are still villages where Greek is spoken and everywhere one sees temples, stadia, and baths recalling the splendors of the Hellenic past.

The Romans were a dynamic people and by the middle of the third century B.C. they were in control of Italy. Through their victories over the Carthaginians their language was carried to Sicily, Spain, and North Africa.

From its beginning Latin had a complex system of case and verb endings. Throughout the years its pronunciation was modified, and through its contact with Greek the vocabulary was enriched. In about 100 B.C. the so-called classical Latin appears—the polished language of Cicero and Virgil. This is the Latin which has been learned by millions of pupils right down to the present day.

Historically, however, this elegant literary Latin did not last much beyond the third century. The lower classes did not spend their time writing polished essays and lofty odes; most of them were illiterate. And in their speech they disregarded the refinements of the grammarians. The system of long and short vowels was ignored; the pronunciation changed. *C,* which had been pronounced like *k* in the classical era, was sounded like *ts* or *ch* before *e* and *i*—a phenomenon evident in present-day Spanish and Italian. The name of the great Roman orator shows the following variant pronunciations: English, Sisero; classical Latin (as taught in our schools), Kikero; French, Seesayron (pronounced like *on* in *wrong*); German, Tseesero; Italian, Chichero; Spanish, Thithero. The Catholic Church tends to follow the Italian pronunciation. *Regina coeli* ("Queen of Heaven"), is pronounced rejeena chelee instead of regheena koilee, with hard *g* and *c,* as in classical Latin.

In the early Middle Ages, case endings in Latin became weaker and prepositions were used more and more. Classical Latin had deteriorated considerably by the fifth century, when the barbarians from the north sacked Rome. Soon thereafter the Roman Empire fell; its demise is dated A.D. 476.

By this time the Latin of the various Roman provinces—Britain, Gaul, Spain, and Lusitania (Portugal)—had been transformed by various local influences. Out of the Vulgar Latin, the speech of the soldiers and the common people, arose the Romance languages—French, Spanish, Portuguese, and Italian.

The first of the daughters of Latin to be clearly identified was French. It was no less a person than Charlemagne who designated the new language. He referred to it as *lingua romana rustica* in an edict of 813, in which he ordered priests to preach in that tongue. In its written form the new language was used on February 14, 842, in the Oaths of Strasbourg, a treaty sworn to by Louis the German and Charles the Bold. This important literary monument, in two languages, documented the separation of France and Germany and of their respective tongues. From then on each went its own way.

The beginnings of Spanish and Italian are placed in the middle of the tenth century. Spanish, which had developed out of Vulgar Latin, was influenced to some extent by the invasions of two foreign groups, the Germanic tribes and the Arabs. The former, who entered the peninsula in A.D. 406, consisted of Suevians, Alans, and Vandals. The Visigoths established their rule from 415 to 755, during which 35 kings occupied the throne. The Arabs dominated Spain for 7 centuries, from 711 to 1492. Despite this, neither the Visigoths nor the Arabs influenced the Spanish language very deeply. The former contributed 300 words, the latter 650.

Germanic tribes also invaded Italy, where they left a much larger proportion of their vocabulary.

However, the foundation of Spanish and Italian, as of all the Romance languages, is definitely Latin. Their resemblance in vocabulary is therefore very close. For example:

English	*Latin*	*French*	*Spanish*	*Portuguese*	*Italian*	*Rumanian*
all	totus	tout	todo	todo	tutto	tot
bread	panis	pain	pan	pao	pane	paine
drink	bibere	boire	beber	beber	bere	bea
good	bonus	bon	bueno	bom	buono	bun
hand	manus	main	mano	mao	mano	mana
life	vita	vie	vida	vida	vita	viata

At this point we might indicate that, with few exceptions, all of the European languages are related and belong to one linguistic family. English, Dutch, German, and the Scandinavian languages constitute the Germanic branch. French, Spanish, Portuguese, Italian, and Rumanian are the Romance languages. The third largest branch is the Slavic; it includes Russian, Polish, Czech, Serbo-Croatian, Slovak, and Slovene. In addition to these major branches there are the Celtic languages—Irish, Scots Gaelic, Welsh, Breton, and Cornish. Greek, Armenian, and Albanian form smaller, separate branches.

All of these languages show resemblances in vocabulary and in structure. Since their common ancestor was the Sanskrit of India, they are called the Indo-European family of languages.

Certain common words are startlingly similar in the various European languages as, for example, Sanskrit *mata,* Greek *meter,* Latin *mater,* Russian *mat,* Irish *mathair,* French *mère,* Spanish *madre,* Italian *madre,* German *Mutter,* English *mother.*

The German philologist Grimm made a study of the changes occurring in the various European languages to explain deviations from Sanskrit. He worked out two sets of philologic laws which are named for him. The first explains the sound shifts from the reconstructed Indo-European tongue to the various European languages; the second shows the transition from Germanic to English.

The Indo-European family includes 7 European and 2 Indian branches. The following table shows the more important languages which make up the nine branches.

The Modern Indo-European Languages

I. Germanic branch

Northern: Icelandic, Danish, Norwegian, Swedish

Western: Dutch, Flemish, Friesian, German, English

II. Italic or Latin branch

The Romance languages: French, Spanish, Portuguese, Catalan, Provençal, Italian, Rumanian

III. Celtic branch

Goidelic: Scots Gaelic, Irish, Manx

Brythonic: Welsh, Breton

IV. Balto-Slavic

Baltic: Lithuanian, Lettish

Slavic: Eastern: Ukrainian, Russian

Western: Polish, Slovak, Czech

Southern: Bulgarian, Serbo-Croatian, Slovene

V. Hellenic branch

Greek

VI. Albanian

VII. Armenian

VIII. Iranian branch

Persian, Kurdish, Balochi, Afghan

IX. Indo-Aryan

Hindi, Urdu, Bengali, Panjabi, Marathi, Gujarati

IN EASTERN EUROPE

Now let us leave Italy and fly to Prague, the capital of Czechoslovakia. There we seem to be at a complete loss, for the language we hear spoken is entirely unrelated to anything we have heard before. Glancing at the signs, we note that the Latin alphabet is used, but certain letters, namely, *c, d, n, r, s, t, z,* have a hook over them to indicate that they are palatalized. The *r* with the hook, for example, is pronounced like trilled *r* together with the *s* of "treasure." Czech resembles Polish and Russian, but the stress is generally on the first syllable of a word. There is no article, but the noun and the adjective are inflected in 7 cases. An accent mark over a vowel indicates that it is long.

Czech is spoken by about 7 million inhabitants of Czechoslovakia; some 3 million speak Slovak. The latter is very close to Czech.

From Prague we can easily reach Warsaw, the capital of Poland. The language spoken there is similar to Czech. Like that language, it uses the Latin alphabet, has seven cases, and no article. However, the stress is on the next to last syllable in most words, hooks are attached below some letters (*a* and *e*) and the letter *w* appears. Another distinguishing feature is its nasal sounds. Polish is the language of the 35,000,000 inhabitants of Poland, some of whom also speak Russian, Ukrainian, German, and Lithuanian. Polish, Czech, and Slovak belong to the Western branch of the Slavic language family. Since the peoples speaking these languages were Christianized from Rome, they use the Latin alphabet.

Belonging to one family, the various Slavic languages resemble one another closely, as shown in the following table. Russian and Bulgarian, which use Cyrillic characters, are given in transliteration.

English	*Polish*	*Czech*	*Russian*	*Serbo-Croatian*	*Bulgarian*
black	czarny	cerny	chorny	crn	cheren
bread	chleb	chleb	chl'eb	hleb	chl'eb
brother	brat	bratr	brat	brat	brat
day	dzien	den	d'en	dan	d'en
drink	pic	piti	peet	piti	peeya
foot	noga	noha	noga	noga	noga
good	dobry	dobry	dobry	dobar	dobr
knife	noz	nuz	nozh	noz	nozh
sea	morze	more	mor'e	more	mor'e
three	trzy	tri	tri	tri	tri
water	woda	voda	voda	voda	voda

A short flight from Warsaw takes us to Kiev, the capital of the Ukraine. There we are faced by difficulties with the written as well as with the spoken language. The Russians use the Cyrillic aphabet, based on Greek, which was given them by two Bishops, Cyril and Methodius, from Byzantium (Constantinople). It has 32 letters, some of which are like ours, but with different values. For example, *B* = *V*, *H* = *N*, *P* = *R*, *C* = *S*, *R* = *Ya*, *N* = *I*. The name "Russia" is written *POCCNR* and is read "Rossiya."

In the Ukraine some 35 million people speak Ukrainian. This is slightly different from standard Russian. The same is true of White Russian, spoken by about 8 million people in west central Russia.

Russian is the official language of the Soviet Union with its 200 million inhabitants. However, only about half speak Russian as their native tongue. Each of the sixteen constituent republics has its own official language. In addition to these, many other languages are spoken, so that the total comes close to 150. There are some 60 ethnic stocks and over a hundred smaller racial groups, each using its own tongue. Among the more important ones are Azerbaijan, Georgian, Armenian, Turcoman, Uzbek, Tadjik, Kazakh, Kirghiz, Korel, Buryat, Tatar, Kalmyk, Mongol Choovash, Bashkir, Mordvin, Osset, Chechen, Circassian, Kabardinian, Abkasian, and Ingush.

The Soviets have not tried to suppress these various languages. Quite the contrary; they have given them every encouragement and have provided with alphabets those that had no written system before. Russian, however, is the official language. Its position has been greatly strengthened by the influx of large numbers of Russians who have gone into Siberia to build up the area industrially and culturally. It is to the advantage of the native to learn Russian. He is, therefore, usually bilingual.

From Leningrad it is only a brief hop to Helsinki, the attractive capital of Finland. Here two languages are spoken, Swedish and Finnish. In fact, in the north there is a third: the language of the Lapps. When we look at the signs the words all seem rather long. There are many double consonants and many double vowels.

As we cross the Baltic and go south through Estonia, Hungary, and to Turkey, we learn that the languages of these countries are all related. They are known as the Ural-Altaic group. Related to them are also languages spoken in Siberia, Turkestan, Mongolia, and Manchuria.

These languages show certain peculiarities that differentiate them from their neighbors. Several suffixes may be added to a root word. A preposition may be inserted between case forms. Nouns have no gender. The geographical position of these languages on the European continent is strange. They form a sort of barrier from north to south between the Slavic and the Germanic groups. The number of speakers is not large: Finnish has 4 million, Estonian, Livonian, and Lapp about 3 million; Hungarian 9 million, and Turkish 20 million.

Let us hasten down to Istanbul, the ancient and picturesque city on the Bosporus, and observe Turkish more closely. Until recently this language was written in Arabic letters, a cumbersome system, since Turkish is not, like Arabic, a Semitic language. Kemal Pasha, the intrepid Turkish leader who democratized the government, reformed the calendar, secularized the schools, and emancipated the women, also modernized the language. He substituted the Roman alphabet for the Arabic and adopted many international words, spelling them phonetically. He accomplished this almost singlehanded, standing daily before a blackboard in a square in Istanbul and explaining his system to the populace. Within a few months he had reformed the Turkish language.

In addition to the adoption of the phonetic alphabet in 1929, the language was simplified by ridding it of many words and expressions of Arabic and Persian origin. A few of the scores of words used in other European languages are now easily recognizable, since they appear in Roman type: *afis, aktör, asfalt, atlet, alkol, barbar, buket, depozito, diploma, doktrin, ekspres, filozof, garanti, konferans, magazin, orkestra, program, problem, radyo, sistem, transit, vagon, vals.*

A short flight from Istanbul brings us to Athens, the capital of Greece. Today it is a little country of 8 million inhabitants, but in ancient times it dominated the civilized world of the

West. Greek was spoken from the Ebro in Spain to the Indus in India. It was the language of art, literature, and philosophy. The New Testament was written in Greek. So many Jews spoke Greek that the Bible was translated for them into that language; the Greek version was known as the Septuagint. Even Latin did not displace Greek in the East when the Romans conquered the Mediterranean, and it remained the language of Constantinople until that city was captured by the Turks in 1453. It has continued to be the language of the Eastern Orthodox Church.

Natives can read Homer and the ancient classics without difficulty but over the centuries the pronunciation has changed so much and so many foreign terms have crept in, that the student of classical Greek will have difficulty in recognizing the spoken language. As in a number of other countries, there is a literary language and a colloquial tongue. The former is close to ancient Greek; the vernacular has simplified some of the more complex grammatical forms. It also contains many words of Turkish origin.

A little country to the northeast of Greece—Albania—speaks a language which was once considered a distinct tongue. Although it has only a million speakers it is divided into two dialects: Gheg and Tosk. About three fifths of the words are borrowed from Turkish, Greek, Latin, and Slavic.

Another language spoken by a small number of speakers and considered a distinct tongue is Armenian. It is heard in eastern Turkey, southwest Russia, and in Asia Minor. It is the smallest member of the European family of languages which we have considered above. This great linguistic category which includes about half the world's population, is comprised of the groups mentioned, namely, the Germanic, Romance, Slavic, Celtic, Greek, Albanian, and Armenian. It is known to philologists as the Indo-European family of language because it is thought that the basic language originated in India. The early speakers moved westward, the language changed, and thus after centuries there evolved Greek, Latin, Russian,

Italian, Spanish, French, German, Dutch, English, and the other European tongues.

Now let us fly over to Africa and go down the western coast. Many new countries have emerged within the last few years, but the culture and the languages of the colonial powers are still in evidence. French, English, Spanish, and Portuguese are widely used, especially by government officials and cultured natives. But the vast majority of Africans speak a large number of diverse tongues.

IN AFRICA

The African Negro languages are grouped in three great divisions: Sudanese-Guinean, Bantu, and Hottentot-Bushman. These are again subdivided into many languages. Some of these have over 2 million speakers.

The extensiveness of the language problem in Africa is realized when we consider that the Dark Continent has a population of over 200 million and that there are 700 different languages. Racially the Africans are divided into Hamites, Negroes, and Bantus. There are 47 Hamitic languages, 182 Bantu languages, 264 Sudanese languages, and 10 Semitic languages. These are again divided and subdivided into dialects, so that there is a veritable babel of tongues in Africa.

It must be pointed out, too, that these are in the main spoken and not written languages. Ghana, which has been independent since March, 1957 and is within the British Commonwealth, has an illiteracy rate of 85 per cent. That is the predominant pattern.

In Ghana, as elsewhere in Africa, a number of languages are used. Although they are spoken by over a million people, their very names are strange to us—Fanti, Ewe, Twi, and Ga.

In Nigeria, the African country largest in population, there are 35 million inhabitants, divided into 250 different tribes. The leading languages are Ibo, Yoruba, Sobo, Bini, Hausa, Fulani, and Kanuri. Of these, Hausa has the largest number of speakers, about 13 million. Ibo has some 3 million.

In British East Africa there is just as great a variety of languages. Each of the 220 tribes speaks its own language. Out of the welter of tongues has come one which is used as the lingua franca of the eastern coast. That is Swahili, which started in the Arab settlements, spread inland, and merged with Bantu. It has about 10 million speakers. It is taught in Howard University in Washington and in Duquesne University.

Uganda, a British protectorate in Central Africa, has a population of about 5 million. The climate is agreeable; social and political conditions are good. There are a number of schools, even a University which is affiliated with the University of London. The national language is Luganda.

In the Union of South Africa, where conditions are not so happy, there are over 8 million Negroes who speak various Bantu languages. Possibly, because of recent news items, the names of two will be recognized—Zulu and Xhosa. The others are quite unknown: Shona, Barotse, Matabele, etc.

In addition to the 8,500,000 Negroes, 1,000,000 Cape Colored (mixed), and 500,000 Asians, there are 2,500,000 Whites. The latter fall into two groups: the English and other European stocks, and the Afrikaanders, the descendants of the original Dutch settlers. The latter speak Afrikaans, which is practically the official language. It has carried the simplifying tendency of Dutch furthest. All the case endings have been sloughed off and the verb uses only a single form throughout the tense. It is interesting to note that Afrikaans has given us "boss" and "trek."

Despite the fact that Africa is rapidly becoming liberated and a dozen states have arisen within the last few years, the shadow of colonialism still lies across the land. This is so particularly with reference to language. Since there are so many tribes and so many languages, government activities are still conducted in the language of the once dominant European power. This means French in North Africa, the Congo, and Equatorial Africa; English in Egypt, the Sudan, the Gold

Coast, and South Africa; Portuguese in Mozambique and Angola.

Flying north across the Dark Continent, we cross vast areas where a myriad of African tongues and dialects are spoken, whose very names look strange. When we reach Cairo, the capital of Egypt, we hear a language which is spoken by 76 million people and whose roots go back to the Tower of Babel. That is Arabic.

When the fanatic hordes of Moslems spread their religion by fire and sword across the lands of the Mediterranean, Arabic became the common idiom from Spain to India. It is still the language of North Africa. Over the centuries, however, the spoken language broke up into numerous dialects, so that the Arabic of Morocco is different from that of Damascus.

Classical Arabic, the literary language, has been preserved unchanged because it is the language of the Koran. In the spoken tongue there are only two genders and no cases. Adjectives follow the noun, object pronouns are attached to the verb. Masculine nouns form their plurals by a vowel change as in English irregular nouns like *goose, geese*. It is interesting to note that such words as alcohol, algebra, alchemy, cipher, zenith, and zero come from the Arabic.

In the Sahara and North Africa the dominant native language is Arabic. At one time the Arabs controlled all of North Africa from the Red Sea to the Strait of Gibraltar. In fact, it was in 711 that the Moslem leader Jebel crossed the strait into Spain. The great rock was named for him, Jebel Tarik—"Tarik's Mountain."

The Arabic spoken in Egypt is somewhat different from that of the east—Jordan, Iraq, and Saudi Arabia—and also from that of the western countries—Libya, Tunisia, Algeria, and Morocco. There are also marked differences between classical and colloquial Arabic, between newspaper and literary Arabic. Since we are in Africa it must be pointed out that some African languages, like Fula, Hausa, and Swahili, often use Arabic characters.

There are in North Africa a number of other languages that must be mentioned. There is Amharic, the language of 5,500,000 Ethiopians, and Mossi, spoken by 5,000,000 people. In French West Africa 120 different languages are spoken.

IN ASIA

From Cairo let us fly to Jerusalem and visit Israel. This is easily done, for it is a small country. There we also hear Arabic, especially in Beersheba in the south and in Nazareth in the north. It is the second language of the country because of the large number of Arabs, many of whom are Christians. The language is used in the *Knesset* (Parliament) and on the Voice of Israel, the official radio station.

Hebrew, however, is the national language of Israel and it is spoken by young and old. Many of the older people, who came from every quarter of the globe, had to make quite an effort to learn it. For a long time a number of the newspapers provided their readers with vocabularies and notes in a half dozen different languages.

Hebrew presents a unique case in linguistic revival and development. Even before the beginning of the Christian era, Hebrew had disappeared from daily life. For centuries it was the language of religion and of Biblical and Talmudic scholarship. Jesus spoke Aramaic, the Palestinian idiom of his time. After the dispersion in A.D. 70, the Jews were scattered all over the world. Two divisions in the pronunciation of Hebrew developed: the Ashkenazic of the North European Jews, and the Sephardic of the Mediterranean Jews. The Ashkenazic pronunciation is still used in the synagogues; the Sephardic pronunciation is the one adopted for the national language of Israel.

Hebrew was revived largely through the indefatigable zeal and relentless perseverance of one man: a poor, consumptive Lithuanian, Eleazar Ben Yehuda. His theory was that the soul of a people is in its language; that no nation can have cultural cohesion without a national tongue. Almost singlehanded, with sheer fanaticism, he won, overcoming the fiercest opposition, chiefly from his own coreligionists. He coined thousands of words and wrote the first volumes of a standard dictionary. It is said that he dropped dead when he reached the word *nafshi,* "soul." He also founded the language committee which has continued his work and built up the vocabulary of the ancient tongue. The Hebrew linguists have worked so well that in the University of Jerusalem the latest scientific findings are now discussed in the tongue of Moses.

Of the several nations that have revived ancient tongues, the Israelis have been the most successful. Hebrew is taught in various parts of the world, including the public schools of New York, Philadelphia, and Chicago. Hebrew is not difficult to acquire, although its alphabet offers some obstacles. The small dots and dashes beside, below, and on top of the consonants represent vowel sounds. These are generally omitted in print in Israel, where it is assumed that the reader is so familiar with the words that he recognizes them without vowels. One difficulty which arises when Hebrew is quoted in the context of a European language, or when Hebrew text is given with musical notation is the fact that it is written from right to left.

Although Arabic uses a different script, it is closely related in vocabulary to Hebrew. These are the two leading languages of the Semitic branch of the Semito-Hamitic languages (Sem and Ham were the sons of Noah; the languages were named for them). This linguistic family includes many languages spoken in North Africa, such as the Amharic of Ethiopia. The modern descendant of ancient Aramaic is Syriac, spoken by Christian groups in Syria, Lebanon, Transjordania, and Iraq.

The flowing script of Arabic is strange and unintelligible to the American tourist but the Hebrew characters seem familiar. He has seen them on numerous signs and store windows in American cities. But there they are not always Hebrew; in fact, they are most often Yiddish.

But let us return to our observation of the Indo-European family of languages. We are familiar with the European branch; now let us look into the "Indo" side. The various members of this family are spread out over southwestern and southern Asia. The languages of Iran, Afghanistan, Baluchistan, and northern India belong to this linguistic group.

The language of Persia, or rather Iran, is no longer purely Indo-European. Many Arabic words have entered the language, which is now written in Arabic characters.

The Pan-American plane takes us to Delhi, the capital of the vast subcontinent of India. In this crowded land of over 400 millions, hundreds of languages are spoken. They fall into two main groups: the Indo-European tongues of the north and the Dravidian languages of the south. There are 16 major languages belonging to the former and 17 belonging to the latter. Besides this there are countless minor dialects.

The question of language is an acute one in India; in fact, the rivalry is so great that it has led to bloodshed. Pakistan and India divided—with the massacre of over 10 million persons—along religious and linguistic lines. Pakistan is Mohammedan; India is Hindu. In West Pakistan the language is Urdu; in the eastern part it is Bengali. In India an attempt is being made to establish Hindi as the national language but much opposition is being encountered. English is still the language of the courts, of Parliament, and of the educated classes. The final solution will probably be a trilingual arrangement. An educated Indian will speak his regional language, will learn the national language, Hindi, at school, and will acquire English for international intercourse.

To give an idea of the welter of tongues in India it must be mentioned that on one of the most widely used notes of currency, the rupee, the amount is given in 5 different languages.

A number of words have entered English from Indian languages, such as yogi, pundit, pajama, curry, chutney, and thug. Aside from such words, the Indian tongues are completely unintelligible to English-speaking persons. Hindi, Bengali, and Urdu are all written in different characters. So are the Dravidian languages like Telugu and Tamil.

The modern Indian languages of the northern part of the country are derived from Sanskrit, a highly complex system. It had 8 cases and complicated tenses, moods, and voices. The modern tongues have simplified all this.

A German philologist, Franz Bopp, during the last century first pointed out the relationship of European languages to ancient Sanskrit, and thereby established the science of comparative philology. As examples of their similarity the following words may be cited:

Indo-Germanic	*Greek*	*Latin*	*English*
ajras	agros	ager	acre
pita	pater	pater	father
mata	mater	mater	mother
yugam	zygon	jugum	yoke
mush	mys	mus	mouse
naktis	nyx	nox	night
trayas	treis	tres	three

From India we fly over Burma, Thailand (Siam), and Tibet. In these countries languages are spoken which are related to Chinese and which belong to the same family.

Let us drop down—vicariously (unless the State Department has relaxed its restrictions)—into Peking. Here we listen to a strange tongue, spoken in a singsong manner, since there are 4 tones in which each word may be pronounced. To the native these tones present no difficulty, but the foreigner can get into all sorts of embarrassing situations by using the wrong one. For example, *ma* means both "mother" and "horse." Conceivably, by using the wrong tone one might ask one's Chinese friend, "How is your horse this morning?" when one really wanted to inquire about the health of his mother.

On the other hand, pronunciation presents no particular

difficulties. There are no unusual or intricate combinations in Chinese. All basic words are of one syllable; they usually end in a vowel or in *n* or *ng*. Chinese lacks some of the sounds of European languages. The number of basic one-syllable words, then, is rather limited. However, Chinese—like German, incidentally—builds up compounds by combining simple words.

Chinese, like English, has many homonyms, that is, words pronounced alike but which have different meanings and which are written differently. In order to avoid ambiguity, Chinese may attach an explanatory word, a so-called classifier.

Since there are no case forms and no parts of speech, the position of a word in a sentence is extremely important. The Chinese say, "I meet she" and "She meet I." There are no inflections, no cases, no personal endings, and no conjugations. Tenses are indicated by adding to the verb the equivalent of "yesterday" (last day) for the past, "today" (this day) for the present, and "tomorrow" (next day) for the future.

The grammar, then, is extremely simple. What is a Herculean task, however, is that of learning the Chinese characters. These ideograms were originally pictures representing an object, an idea, an act, or a situation. "Sun" was represented by a drawing of a circle with rays; the picture for "moon" looked like the moon. Gradually they became conventionalized. Many of the ideograms are quite intricate, requiring 16 or more strokes of the brush to write. Fortunately, there are only 214 basic characters, but these can be combined so that the staggering total of 40,000 is reached. Only about 4,000, however, are in general use; but that is plenty!

These symbols are the same for all of the 450 million Chinese, but the pronunciation is not uniform. The language has been broken up into numerous dialects which are mutually incomprehensible. The chief forms of Chinese are Mandarin, the "national tongue," and Cantonese, Wu, and Min.

The Communists are trying to simplify the language by reducing the number of symbols. There is even a movement on foot to introduce the Roman alphabet in place of the cumbersome and intricate Chinese characters.

Chinese belongs to the Sino-Tibetan family of languages which includes Burmese, Thai, and Tibetan. This group of languages counts over 500 million speakers—practically one fourth of the human race.

Let us now board our plane again and hop to Tokyo. The capital of Japan is a Westernized city with tall office buildings, department stores, much traffic, and a subway. The signs seem to be in Chinese characters. That is true. The Japanese adopted the Chinese ideographs in the eighth century, although the two languages are not related.

Chinese is monosyllabic; Japanese is polysyllabic. Tones are not used in Japanese. Stress is evenly distributed; vowels are long or short. Pronouns which are important in Chinese are practically discarded in Japanese.

Whereas the Chinese verb is extremely simple, it is quite complicated in Japanese. There are many intricate familiar and polite forms. The latter are particularly involved. The very words for husband, wife, son, etc., differ according to whether one is referring to the members of one's own family or to those of the person spoken to. Another unreasonable complication is involved in the use of numbers. There are two sets. One set is borrowed from the Chinese; the other is strictly Japanese. The words for the numbers change their form depending upon the type of noun they qualify—a human being, an animal, a round object, a square object, etc.

The biggest obstacle—and what an obstacle it is!—is the system of writing. The Japanese have copied many things successfully from other nations, but their taking over of the Chinese ideographs was a disaster. The Chinese characters are entirely unsuited to the Japanese language. Since Japanese is inflected, some way had to be devised to show changes in form and endings. So the Chinese ideographs were modified by adding characters representing sounds. The Japanese system of writing thus became a mixture of Chinese ideographs plus phonetic script called *kana*. The latter represented the sounds of certain grammatical particles. Difficult words are often explained in parallel phonetic script. What finally happened was that not one but many systems of writing evolved. Thus the written form of Japanese is fearfully unwieldy and inefficient. Japanese can be written in a dozen different ways, in various mixtures of characters, and in what are known as phonetic syllabaries. Different forms are used in newspapers, legal documents, technical studies, and literary works. In addition, there are 4 different styles of writing: the vernacular, the literary, the epistolary, and the commercial. Furthermore, the characters can be written vertically, horizontally, from right to left, or from left to right. The multiplicity of readings is bewildering: some words can be pronounced with 80 different sounds.

Learning to read and write is a colossal task, especially handwriting. Characters are written with as many as 48 brush strokes; 20 are common. Thousands of characters have to be memorized; to read philosophy a knowledge of tens of thousands is required. The cultured Japanese is never finished learning his native language.

The complexity of the writing systems interferes with the efficient use of typewriters, linotype machines, filing systems, and duplicating processes. A Japanese *kanji* typewriter has 2,005 characters, plus a reservoir of 858 in the rare-type drawer! Imagine being a typist in a Japanese office!

All this goes to show how a language may become a real cultural barrier and cut off a people intellectually from the rest of the world. Various efforts have been made to simplify the written system. A movement is now on foot to Romanize written Japanese.

HOME AGAIN

Let us fly from Tokyo across the Pacific to Anchorage, Alaska. We are in the New World again. English is the language here and in Canada. That is, with one great exception. In the eastern part, in Quebec, French is the tongue of the people. These are the French-Canadians. They have held on tenaciously to their language and culture and religion since the days of Champlain.

But let us continue down the west coast. In California we encounter many Spanish place names—San Francisco, Santa Barbara, Monterey, etc.—reminiscent of the fact that the conquistadors discovered this region.

Spanish is widely spoken in the Southwest. In fact, one may consider New Mexico bilingual. There are also other languages than English spoken by smaller groups: the German of the Mennonites of Kansas, the Russian of the Molokans of Arizona, besides the dialects of the Indians. There are about 250,000 Indians in the Southwest speaking about 65 different tongues.

Indian languages have been preserved much better in Latin America. In Mexico almost a million Indians still speak the tongue of their Aztec ancestors. Many Indians do not speak Spanish. An enterprising publisher has devised a unique and successful way of teaching them the national language by means of comic books.

There are many Indian languages. Those that have larger numbers of speakers are the Quechua in Peru, Aymara in Bolivia, and Tupi-Guarani in Paraguay. Quechua and Guarani are considered important enough to be taught in the public schools. Many whites have learned these languages in order to be able to deal with the Indians.

The tongue of Castile is, however, the dominant language from the Rio Grande south. It is the official language of all of the 21 Latin-American republics except Brazil, which speaks Portuguese, and Haiti, which speaks French.

Much fuss is made over the *seseo* by our language teachers, that is, the pronunciation of soft *c* as *s* and not as *th* as in standard Castilian. The difference is so slight that it is negligible. There are also some variations in pronunciation, like the Spanish of Buenos Aires which has been influenced by the large numbers of Italians in that city. But on the whole the spoken language throughout South America is quite uniform. We have no difficulty with our high school Spanish in Bogotá, Lima, Santiago, Buenos Aires, and Montevideo.

Portuguese, the language of Brazil, does not offer a barrier either, for it is similar to Spanish.

Finally, let us return to our native land, after this kaleidoscopic jaunt through the world's languages. We step off the plane at Idlewild and immediately, before we hear a word of English, we listen to a welter of Spanish, Italian, German, Yiddish, Polish. Yes, we are in New York, the world's most polyglot city.

And as we drive through Manhattan, we see signs in a dozen different languages; we pass Armenian, Japanese, Indian, Mexican, Indonesian, Swedish, French, Dutch, and Danish restaurants. If we get off for lunch at the Empire State Building, we will find a large and colorful Bavarian restaurant in the basement, with a complete Munich atmosphere from the Löwenbräu and sauerbraten to the musicians in *Lederhosen,* who sing lusty drinking songs in their native dialect.

Continuing on our way through the city we hear foreign tongues all around us—much Spanish, of the Puerto Rican variety, and a good deal of Yiddish. This is not strange, for almost half of the 12 million Jews in the world live in the United States. The largest concentration is in New York where 2 daily newspapers and innumerable periodicals and books are published in Yiddish. Over 40 Yiddish schools are maintained by the Workmen's Circle.

Of course, not all Jews speak Yiddish, but most of them know some words or expressions in this tongue. It is, after all, the great repository of Jewish folklore, poetry, and humor. Some of the finest literary works from the hands of Jewish authors have been written in Yiddish. One need only think of so brilliant a writer as Sholom Asch. The works of this author refute the assertion often made that Yiddish is not a language. Actually, it has one of the richest vocabularies and can match any modern tongue in flexibility and versatility.

Yiddish is heard in most of the large cities of the United States. It is also heard in Buenos Aires, since there are 400,000 Jews in the Argentine capital. Over 2 million Jews are in the Soviet Union, and it is there that Yiddish flourished until it was suppressed by the Communists.

Yiddish is also spoken in South Africa, in Australia, and in England and France. The most important center of Yiddish cultural activities in Europe is now Paris. But Yiddish is only one of the many foreign tongues spoken in the United States. We do not have to leave home to hear foreign languages.

America is multilingual.

After this rapid review of the world's languages, you may heave a sigh of exhaustion and feel completely helpless in the face of this welter of tongues. Communication with the rest of the world does seem to be a staggering problem. Experts have estimated that there are about 3,000 different languages! This figure does not even include the numerous subdivisions, variants, and dialects.

Actually, one need not become discouraged; most of the 3,000 languages are, as far as we are immediately concerned, of no importance for world communication. Let us consider our nearest contacts.

English is spoken throughout the United States and Canada (except Quebec, where French is the language). Spanish is the language of all the Latin-American republics except Brazil, whose language is Portuguese, and Haiti, which uses French. In the Western Hemisphere, then, the problem is simple: Spanish, French, and possibly Portuguese will do beautifully.

When we turn to Europe, the situation is somewhat more complicated, for on that little continent almost two dozen languages with rich cultural backgrounds are spoken. Again, most of them cannot be considered world languages, regardless of their contributions to the arts or to literature. Danish, for instance, has only 4 million speakers. With reference to number of speakers, political and industrial importance of the country where the language is spoken, and the closeness of our relations, we can get along rather well with five languages, namely, French, German, Italian, Spanish, and Russian. The first two are spoken by cultured people and by waiters, hotel people, and officials almost everywhere. Fortunately, the first four languages have been taught in our schools for a long time, so that we do have many fellow citizens who can handle one or the other fairly well. Russian, of course, is a newcomer, but within a few years we ought to have a considerable number of Americans who can speak *po-Russky*.

When we reach Asia, we are confronted by linguistic walls. Fortunately for the American traveler and businessman, most cultured people, especially in India, in the Arabic countries, in Hong Kong, and Japan, speak English. But what languages should our Johnny learn if he is to play a role in Asiatic affairs?

The language with the largest number of speakers and the language of the country which will undoubtedly be of vast significance to the world within a few years, is Chinese. It has 545,000,000 speakers! It is the most widely spoken language on the face of the globe, for every fourth human being is a Chinese. Now, those who would disparage the importance of Chinese stress the fact that it is broken up into dialects and that the native from the south cannot understand the native from the north. That is true, but the important fact is that the written language, the Chinese pictograms, are the same for everybody. In other words, all Chinese can read the same script, even though they may pronounce it differently. Furthermore, earnest efforts are now being made to simplify and standardize the language. A Romanized alphabet is being considered. What this will mean, in view of China's enormous industrial potential, her ability to undersell all competitors in Asia, and the fact that businessmen in Southeast Asia are largely Chinese, is overpowering. Chinese should be first on our list of exotic languages.

Another Asiatic country with a huge population and an unexplored potential is India. In our struggle for world stability and security, we will probably have to rely primarily on this vast subcontinent. As was pointed out in our flight around the world, it is a land of many tongues. In fact, some 300 languages have been identified. The government is making strenuous efforts to establish Hindi as the official language and at present over 40 per cent of the population uses it. This, then, should be the second "exotic" language to be studied by specialists and experts who plan to serve in Asia.

Possibly Japanese, which counts 95,000,000 speakers, should also be included, as well as Malay with 70,000,000, and Bengali with 80,000,000.

However, because of the crucial situation in the Near East, the question of oil, and the vast influence of the Moslem world, Arabic should also be considered. As has been pointed out, it is the language of Islam and extends from Morocco across North Africa, through the Near East to China, India, Indonesia, and the East Indies. It is spoken by 76 million people.

The number of important world languages, then, comes down to about a dozen. In fact, aside from English there are only 12 languages with more than 50 million speakers. These are:

Chinese	545,000,000	Bengali	79,000,000
Hindi	149,000,000	Portuguese	74,000,000
Russian	156,000,000	Arabic	76,000,000
Spanish	142,000,000	French	70,000,000
German	120,000,000	Malay	69,000,000
Japanese	95,000,000	Italian	57,000,000

Six of these are being taught in our schools. The other 6, predominantly Asiatic tongues, should be offered in special high schools and colleges.

WHY NOT ONE LANGUAGE FOR THE WHOLE WORLD?

Long ago it was realized that the existence of so many languages and dialects created cultural barriers and prevented free communication. The prevalence of so many tongues is costly, unreasonable, and wasteful. Languages, like living organisms, develop, flourish, decline, and die. Within historic times, Greek and Latin have become dead languages. There are many extinct tongues which philologists have not yet been able to unravel. Actually, there have always been two tendencies, one toward the reduction of the number of languages and the other toward their increase. As the various West European nations became unified, one of the many dialects spoken within the country was raised to the level of the official, standard, and literary language. In France, it was the French of the Île de France; in Italy it was Tuscan; in Spain it was the language of Castile; in Germany it stemmed from Luther's translation of the Bible. The other languages within each country disappeared or dropped to the level of dialects.

The predominance of a given language in any age and in any part of the world is directly related to the size, power, and cultural influence of the country to which it is native. Throughout history, various languages have been leading languages in the Western world. Through the conquests of Alexander, Greek became the language of the civilized world. Later, the Romans established Latin as the universal tongue of Europe and the Near East. It continued during the Middle Ages to be the language of the church and of the scholars. The dominance of France in politics and culture made French the universal language of Europe. Today the nearest approach to a world language is English.

No one language, however, has ever been accepted in all parts of the globe. Those who have concerned themselves with the problem have offered one of three possible solutions. These are:

1. The creation of an artificial, universal language, to be used as an auxiliary for world communication.

2. The designation of one of the living languages—say, English, French, German, or Spanish—as a world language.

3. The division of the world into several linguistic areas, in each one of which one or a number of languages would be considered the dominant one for international use.

The assumption in each case is, of course, that all the countries of the world would agree on the language selected and would teach it in their schools. Unfortunately, getting all human beings to speak one language is about as likely to succeed as persuading them to accept one religion!

Many distinguished linguists and brilliant thinkers have tried to construct an international language. Since the seventeenth century over 500 of them have been evolved. Of all of these only one has achieved any notable success. That is Esperanto, published in 1887 by Dr. Zamenhof. It is used by international associations, is taught in the public schools of some countries, is broadcast on some foreign stations, and is used in 100 magazines and newspapers. Despite this, it probably can count no more than 100,000 speakers.

An interesting development among recent attempts at an artificial language is Interlingua, a simplified Latin intended primarily for the publication and the reading of scientific material. This is obviously useful to those who have Latin, but excludes the vast areas of Asia and Africa where Latin is unknown.

The hitch in all the artificial languages is that they are based on a given number of West European language families —generally, Romance and Germanic—and ignore the languages of China, India, and the Far East. It is practically impossible to devise a language which will be equally easy for all speakers. Furthermore, an artificial language will be subject to the same laws as a living language; variations in pronunciation will soon arise, which, if unimpeded, will lead to the formation of dialects. Before long, the universal language would break up into many variants, quite as unintelligible as different languages.

The designation of one of the living languages for world use seems reasonable enough. The trouble is, however, that men are not moved by reason but rather by emotion. The attachment to one's language is more than mere habit or sentiment. It involves the deepest feelings, the most sacred traditions. Language is part of one's cultural heritage; it is the repository of the aspirations, sufferings, sentiments, and ideals of a people. Hence, a nation clings to its language as to its flag. To ask it to give up its native tongue, or to relegate that to a minor place, is like asking it to change its religion. National pride refuses to concede the superiority of another tongue.

The third solution offered—that of dividing the world into linguistic areas—appears most likely to succeed. It would not require world agreement, it would not offend national pride, and it would be the most practical arrangement. In fact, it is already in operation, for it is a natural process.

As was pointed out above, in the Western Hemisphere there are two dominant languages: English and Spanish. Of lesser usefulness are French and Portuguese. That makes it rather simple: Americans and Canadians will learn Spanish; Latin Americans will learn English as a first language. French and Portuguese would be second languages.

As was shown in the chapter summarizing the languages taught in European schools, English, French, and German are the dominant languages of Western Europe. As second languages, Spanish, Italian, and Russian would be useful.

In Eastern Europe Russian is the major language. As we move East, the linguistic areas would include Arabic, Hindi, Chinese, Japanese, Bengali, Malay, and Indonesian. In each of the Asiatic countries a European language of world importance, such as English, French, or German, should also be offered.

With some modifications, this is exactly what is happening.

Millions of Asians are learning English and French and German. They are learning these languages so well that they can pursue scholarly work at European universities and publish works of distinction. Nehru not only speaks several Indian languages; he speaks and writes a beautiful English. There are many educated Indians and Japanese who can do the same. In Japan, English is begun in the fifth grade.

What about our Johnny? Is he going to continue with his meager fare of two years of Spanish or French?

7 · Where Do We Go from Here?

STARTLED and shocked by the continued achievements of the Soviets in science, by their successes in international relations, and by the intensive training given their specialists, Washington finally decided to act.

In August of 1958, the National Defense Education Act (Public Law 85–864) was passed by Congress and signed by the President on September 2. It authorized something over a billion dollars in Federal aid over a four year period to improve education in schools and colleges. Under ten "titles" it provided for the stimulation of every level of learning from grade school to university.

The Act reflected a rather unique and revolutionary idea. Up to this time it had been assumed that the Cold War meant military rivalry and diplomatic maneuvering. But from a careful study of the Soviet system, its aims and methods, had emerged the grandiose idea that we had to meet the Soviet threat to dominate the world not by bombs but by brains. In the words of the Act itself, it was "to insure trained manpower of sufficient quality and quantity to meet the national defense needs of the United States."

The specific title covering foreign languages is No. VI, "Language Development." Part A provides up to 8 million dollars to set up centers for research and studies, and Part B 7¼ million dollars for language institutes. The latter are to offer advanced training to language teachers. Those attending get weekly stipends of $75 plus $15 for each dependent. The institutes, generally held in the summer, are connected with colleges and universities. In addition to this, another title provides millions for the audio-visual devices and the setting up of language laboratories.

This is all very encouraging but it hasn't, up to this moment, made a single basic change in our foreign language teaching in the high schools. Millions are being spent on audio-visual devices and on language labs which the average teacher is not trained to use. The new devices are expensive and complicated. The kids are thrilled by the novelty of the machinery; the teachers are bewildered as to how to fit the electronic device into the daily lesson. The enthusiasts claim it will now be possible to turn out linguists in short order. The tape recorder threatens to replace the teacher.

The recording devices and the microphones do make possible much additional practice, it is true. They are not, however, equally useful for initiating a new lesson. Their great weakness is that the student's errors are not immediately corrected. Reliance has to be placed on his own ability to detect his mistakes by comparison with the model.

The tape does reproduce the human voice with amazing accuracy. It is now possible, too, to introduce the voices of native speakers into the classroom. This will be particularly beneficial in the case of class teachers whose own pronunciation is none too good.

There are wonderful potentialities in the use of the audio-visual devices. But they cannot replace the personality of the live teacher. They are, at best, useful teaching aids.

The orthophonic device has already become so dominant that it is unconsciously influencing the methodology and the very philosophy of language teaching. Overwhelming emphasis is placed on the audio (the visual plays a minor role). The drill exercise, with its numerous repetitions by the student, brings back learning by imitation. The single, detached sentence, too, reappears; it is the unit for practice. The danger of monotony is not absent. It will take some time and effort to determine the optimum use of the language laboratory. It may prove to be a very effective device.

However, aside from the use of audio-visual devices, the installation of some language laboratories—chiefly in colleges and universities—and the introduction of foreign language instruction in the grade schools of some communities, the foreign language situation in the United States is pretty much as it has been. The length of the course has not been increased. The foreign language is still an elective subject. Extremely few colleges have increased their entrance requirements with respect to foreign languages. In the great majority of the states no teacher training institution offers a modern language.

What have we been trying to stress in the foregoing pages? The absolute inadequacy of our foreign language program in the face of world conditions.

The study of foreign languages is the weakest subject in our educational system. Half the public high schools do not offer it, most students pursue it for only two years.

Because of the position of leadership of the United States in the Western world, the need for a widespread and thorough knowledge of foreign languages among our people is urgent. Linguistic competence has become one of the major weapons in the struggle for survival.

That competence is definitely required in the following areas.

Military. Our armed forces are found all over the world. Of the total of 3 million, 1,370,000 are stationed abroad. We have bases in every quarter of the globe. The personnel of these military establishments cannot function effectively without a knowledge of the language spoken in the country where the men are stationed. In fact, they are helpless in certain situations. Not too long ago an American sergeant was robbed of his payroll in broad daylight in Paris. Despite the presence of many pedestrians, this officer was unable to secure help because he could not say "*Au secours!* (Help!)" or "*Au voleur!* (Stop thief!)."

On the battlefield the knowledge of the meaning of one word in the foreign language has helped to save the lives of scores of men.

Commanding officers are now issuing directives requiring their men to learn the language of the country in which they are serving. This is to be commended; but how much more economical and efficient it would be if the men had been taught the language in the United States, during their days in high school or college.

In view of the present political and military constellation in Europe, there is absolutely no doubt that French and German are badly needed by our armed forces. Hundreds of thousands of men are stationed in France and Germany; these are the bastions to be held against Communism in the event of war. It is surprising that the Army has not stressed this fact and urged that school authorities train the young men who will soon enlist in knowledge of these languages.

German is the most widely studied language among our forces abroad. At home less than one per cent of the high school population takes that language. And, for obvious reasons, much more attention should be given to Russian.

The whole question is neither academic nor insignificant. In fact, the number of persons involved is huge. During World War I almost 2,400,000 served in foreign parts; in the second World War it was almost 11,500,000. And in the Korean conflict of 1950–53 about 3,700,000 Americans were involved. There are constantly about 3 million men in the armed forces.

The military authorities are now keenly aware of the fact that language competence is important. In 1954, the United States Air Force organized a mandatory, on-duty program in foreign languages for all personnel in Europe. Every encouragement is given the men to go beyond the required courses which are offered in ten languages. Here in the States members of the Air Force are being trained in the Army Language School and in a number of universities.

In the Air Force Academy the study of a foreign language is required. This is true also of West Point and of Annapolis. There are also the Counter-Intelligence Corps school of the Army and the Navy's foreign language school in Anacostia. In the Army's language school at Monterey, California, 31 foreign languages are taught. There is an enrollment of 2,400 students. At SHAPE (Supreme Headquarters Allied Powers, Europe) a language laboratory was set up in 1953.

The attitude of the Army toward language study is well expressed by Gen. Matthew B. Ridgway, who said, when he was Chief of Staff:

> The value of a knowledge of foreign languages is nowhere more apparent than in the military profession . . . I am convinced that increasing our knowledge of foreign languages will add significantly to our national security . . .

Diplomacy. If there ever was a period in our history when a knowledge of foreign languages was urgently needed, in diplomatic affairs, it is now. Our world relations have been going from bad to worse. The Cold War is becoming icy; the Japanese riot in protest against our policies; Castro denounces us with impunity; Iceland is cool; Latin America is sullen; and even England is sour. Our envoys are hooted and showered with stones.

Now, some, if not all of this ill feeling might have been avoided if our representatives had been able to confer with the leaders of foreign nations in their own language. It is beyond any doubt that Vice President Nixon would have been received courteously, if not cordially, had he been able to say a few words in Spanish during his South American trip. How different was the reception which Secretary Herter got in Paris and Bonn because he spoke both French and German!

One may even claim that the relations between the United States and the Soviet Union would be different today if Stalin and Khrushchev had been able to speak English and Roosevelt and Eisenhower had been able to speak Russian.

If we are to achieve a greater measure of success in our diplomatic relations, we must see to it that our representatives speak foreign languages. This means not only the commoner European languages but the tongues of the Far East and of Africa.

Fifteen new nations have evolved out of colonies on the Dark Continent within recent years, and each one seeks to preserve its traditions and its culture. If we are to control the situation there, and not lose it to the Soviets, we must teach African languages, at least to our specialists. At present very few of them are taught at any of our colleges and universities.

Hausa, a language of Central Africa, has 13 million speakers, Swahili has 8 million, Amharic 6, and Mossi 5. Yet none of these is taught at any of our universities. The same thing is true of Javanese, with 41 million speakers, and the following languages of India, each of which has more than 13 million speakers: Marathi, Gujarati, Rajasthani, Kanarese, Malayalam and Oriya.

Foreign Trade. During the last few years our exports and imports have been increasing tremendously. However, we cannot sit back and regard the figures complacently. There are determined and vigorous competitors in the offing.

The Japanese, whose production costs are so much lower than ours, have been flooding the market with cameras, transistor radios, machine goods, and textiles. Such great quantities of clothing have been imported from Nippon that our clothing workers unions have risen in protest. The Japanese worker gets 14 cents an hour; the American gets about two dollars.

An even greater threat in Asia comes from China, which can draw on a vast and minutely controlled industrial potential.

To maintain our present business supremacy we will have to gear our products to the needs of the foreign customer and to speak his language. Our competitors have done that for a long time. British, French, and German firms are building huge plants in South America. Their representatives know the people and know the language.

It is evident, then, that Johnny should learn a foreign language. *A* foreign language? Nay, at least two.

As was pointed out above, the world can be divided into certain linguistic areas in each of which two or three languages are dominant, and which are used for international communication.

Which languages are to be offered in our schools?

For how long are they to be studied?

If we look again at the courses of study of European schools, we will see that a first language is generally begun in the first grade of the secondary school. It is pursued for 7–9 years. A second language is begun in the third or the fourth year.

Applying this to our own system, the student would begin his first foreign language in the seventh grade of junior high school and continue it through high school, thus giving him six years. He would start the second language with his entry into senior high school and study it for three years. This formal instruction should be preceded by several years of informal oral activities in the elementary school.

In order to give foreign languages real status and a firm footing in the American high school curriculum, they should be made a required subject, at least for the academic diploma. It is a disgrace—and a deception!—when one considers that thousands of youngsters can graduate from a large metropolitan high school and get a diploma merely for having occupied a seat for 3 or 4 years. They have never had any real science, any real math, and absolutely no foreign language.

Both languages taken in high school would be continued in college. This would give the student a thorough mastery.

Again, two languages should be required for the academic diploma, and at least one for the commercial diploma.

European schools preserve the distinction between the

classical and the mathematics "side." This might be done in our schools, too. Latin should be a required subject for the B.A.

A foreign language should also be a required subject in teacher training institutions. How can we expect foreign languages to have any standing as a school subject if even the teachers are without it? At this writing, there are only two teachers colleges in the State of New York that offer a foreign language. In most states no teachers training school at all teaches a foreign language.

As shown previously, the world's most widely spoken languages, besides English, are only 12 in number—6 European and 6 Asiatic. We ought, then, to strengthen our teaching of French, German, Italian, and Spanish. Russian can be added in a number of schools.

The Asiatic languages, since they will be primarily for the specialist and the Foreign Service officer, should be offered in special language schools in larger cities, and in colleges.

It is interesting to note that whereas schools and colleges have been slow in providing for what is a real need, commercial enterprises have done so. Large corporations with extensive foreign connections pay to have their personnel equipped with the languages required.

One of the best-known and most successful of the private language schools is Berlitz School of Languages. It has branches all over the world. The 27 schools in the United States are attended by about 25,000 persons a year. Berlitz publishes basic texts in more than 30 languages. The school also teaches English. In fact, that is its chief source of revenue in foreign countries. It has had contracts for the teaching of English with several governments, including such remote countries as Indonesia.

The Latin-American Institute makes a specialty of training bilingual secretaries and export personnel for service in firms dealing with South America.

Tens of thousands of adults have learned a foreign language

by the use of records. There are now a score of companies in this thriving business. One of the most widely known is Linguaphone, whose sales amount to over 2 million dollars annually. It provides courses in 34 languages. The 5 languages which constitute 80 per cent of the sales are Spanish (50 per cent), French, German, Japanese, and Russian. English records make up 70 per cent of their sales abroad. It is interesting to note that while years ago British English was the most popular, American English (they have a separate set of records) is now almost universally used. Japan imports only American English records and tapes.

This widespread and increasing interest in the learning of foreign languages, for which so many private enterprises provide, should finally stir the professional educators to action.

A vital factor in the situation is the attitude of the colleges. The greatest damage was done when the language requirements for admission were reduced and even dropped entirely. Formerly, any self-respecting institution of higher learning required several years of a language. In New York City it was 3 years of one language and 2 of another. This meant that a student frequently offered a classical language in addition to a modern language. As one school official described the change: "When I entered Princeton I had had 2 years of Greek and 4 of French; last week my son was admitted with 2 years of Spanish."

Fortunately, the tide is turning. The trend has changed, but it is changing slowly and very mildly. It was considered a great achievement recently when Columbia announced that 3 years of a foreign language would now be required for admission. Three years? It should be at least 4, and 2 or 3 of a second language. Yes, of a second one. It is amazing that even the leaders in the field of foreign language have hardly mentioned the idea of requiring a second language. "Better competence in one than a smattering of two!" Why not competence in two? If young people in Switzerland and Sweden, Norway and the Netherlands can learn 2 and 3 foreign languages well, why not young Americans? The colleges can bring this about by restoring the admission requirement of 2 languages.

Another thing that can be done on the upper level to strengthen language instruction is strict adherence to the language requirement for the Ph.D. degree. It would seem to be perfectly reasonable to expect anyone who plans to do research to be able to read a foreign language. Yet many institutions do not require it. California has even passed a law forbidding it!

In short, our foreign language program will amount to something only if foreign language instruction is begun in the grades, if the high schools require 6 years of a first language and three of a second for the academic diploma, and if the colleges require 6 years of one language and 3 of a second for admission. If that is done, we will have something that can face up to the challenge of Soviet education.

In fact, we must do it soon if we hope to maintain our political, economic, military, and cultural leadership in the world. Otherwise we will be snowed under by more alert, determined, and indefatigable rivals.

For the sake of his personal enrichment, his advancement in his career, and his effectiveness as an intelligent American citizen—

JOHNNY SHOULD LEARN FOREIGN LANGUAGES!

Bibliography

Andersson, Theodore: *The Teaching of Foreign Languages in the Elementary School,* Boston, Heath, 1953.

Huebener, Theodore: *How To Teach Foreign Languages Effectively,* New York, New York Univ. Press, 1959.

———: *Opportunities in Foreign Languages,* New York, Vocational Guidance Manuals, 1955.

———: *Audio-Visual Techniques in Teaching Foreign Languages,* New York, New York Univ. Press, 1960.

Matthew, Robert John: *Language and Area Studies in the Armed Services—Their Future Significance,* Washington, D.C., American Council on Education, 1947.

Newmark, Maxim: *Twentieth Century Modern Language Teaching,* New York, Philosophical Library, 1948.

Parker, William R.: *The National Interest and Foreign Languages,* U.S. National Commission for UNESCO, Department of State, 1949.

Pei, Mario: *One Language for the World,* New York, Devin-Adair, 1953.

———: *Language for Everybody,* New York, Devin-Adair, 1957.

———: *The Story of Language,* Philadelphia, Lippincott, 1949.

———: *Languages for War and Peace,* New York, Vanni, 1943.

Index

Abkasian, 97
Advertising, foreign languages in, 65
Afghan, 95, 105
Africa, languages in, 81, 100–103
  missionaries in, 60
  U.S. trade with, 45
African languages, in U.S. schools, 79
Afrikaans, 85, 101
Airlines, foreign languages in, 51
Alabama, foreign language study in, 38
Alans, 93
Alaska, language in, 109
Albanian, 94, 95, 99
  radio programs in, 69
Algeria, language in, 102
  missionaries in, 60
Alsace, language in, 86
America (*see* United States)
Amharic, 103, 104, 124
Andersson, Theodore, 19
Angola, language in, 102
Arabic, 98, 102, 103, 104, 117
  dominance of, 114
  in French schools, 27
  radio programs in, 56, 69, 70
  in Russian schools, 35
  in U.S. schools, 37
Arabs, 93
  U.S. trade with, 44
Aragonese, 90
Aramaic, 103
Argentina, foreign language study in, 36
  international broadcasting services of, 69
  missionaries in, 60
  U.S. trade with, 44
Arizona, foreign language study in, 38
Arkansas, foreign language study in, 38
Armed forces, foreign language studies in, 78, 121
Armenian, 94, 95, 97, 99
  radio programs in, 55, 69
  spoken in U.S.A., 72, 111
Army Language School, 54
Army Specialized Training Program, 16
Ashkenazic, 103
Asia, 103–109
  linguistic difficulties in, 113
  missionaries in, 61
  U.S. trade with, 44
Audio-visual devices, 16, 120
Australia, foreign language study in, 36

Australia—(*Continued*)
international broadcasting services of, 69
U.S. trade with, 45
Austria, foreign language study in, 24, 36
language of, 86
Austrians, in U.S.A., 1
Aymara, 110
Azerbaijan, 97
Aztecs, 110

Balochi, 95
Baltic languages, 95
Baluchistan, language of, 105
Banking, foreign languages in, 49
Bantu, 100, 101
Barotse, 101
Bashkir, 97
Basque, 89
Bavaria, language in, 85
Beersheba, language of, 103
Belgium, language of, 84
U.S. trade with, 44
Ben Yehuda, Eleazar, 103
Bengali, 95, 105, 114, 117
Berlitz School of Languages, 126
Bini, 100
Bokmal, 86
Bolivia, language in, 110
missionaries in, 60
Bopp, Franz, 106
Brazil, foreign language study in, 36
language of, 90, 110
missionaries in, 60
radio stations in, 66
U.S. trade with, 44, 48
Breton, 82, 88, 94, 95
British (*see* Englishmen)
Broadcasts in foreign languages, 9, 55, 65, 66, 69
Voice of America, 55, 77
Brythonic, 82, 95
Bulgarian, 95
Burma, foreign language study in, 36
Burmese, 106, 108
Buryat, 97

California, foreign language study in, 38
Canada, international broadcasting services of, 69
language in, 110
U.S. trade with, 44
Canadians, in U.S.A., 1
Cantonese, 107
Castilian, 90, 110, 115
Catalan, 90, 95
Celtic languages, 82, 94, 95
Central America, U.S. trade with, 44
Ceylon, foreign language study in, 36
language in, 81
Chechen, 97
Chile, missionaries in, 60
radio stations in, 66
U.S. trade with, 44
Chinese, 106, 117
in department stores, 71
dominance of, 113
in libraries, 71
in private language schools, 8, 37
radio programs in, 69
in Russian schools, 35
translators needed for, 75
in United Nations, 77
in U.S. schools, 16
Circassian, 97
Civil Service, bilingual employees in, 73
regional offices of, 76
Coleman Report, 13
Colleges, foreign language courses in, 79, 127
Colombia, missionaries in, 60
U.S. trade with, 44

Colorado, foreign language study in, 38
Congo, language in, 101
missionaries in, 60
U.S. trade with, 45
Connecticut, foreign language study in, 19, 38
Consuls, training of, 42–43, 51–58, 73, 124
Cornish, 82, 89, 94
Correspondence, in foreign languages, 65, 72, 73, 77
Correspondents, foreign, 67
Corsican, 91
Croatian, in libraries, 71
Cuba, missionaries in, 60
radio stations in, 66
U.S. trade with, 44, 48
Cymric, 82
Cyrillic alphabet, 59, 96
Czech, 94, 95
in libraries, 71
in private language schools, 8, 37
radio programs in, 69
translators needed for, 75
in U.S. colleges, 79
Czechoslovakia, international broadcasting services of, 69
Czechoslovakians, in U.S.A., 1, 72

Danish, 86, 94
in libraries, 71
in private language schools, 8
spoken in U.S.A., 71, 111
teaching of, 25
translators needed for, 75
in U.S. colleges, 79
Delaware, foreign language study in, 38
Denmark, foreign language study in, 25–26, 36
Department stores, foreign languages in, 71
Derthick, L. G., 34
Diplomats, training of, 42–43, 51–58, 73, 123
Dominican Republic, foreign language study in, 36
Dravidian languages, 105
Dutch, 84, 94
in libraries, 71
publications in, 66
radio programs in, 69
scientific abstracts in, 70
in secretarial work, 72
spoken in U.S.A., 71, 111
teaching of, 29
translators needed for, 75
in U.S. colleges, 79
(*See also* Netherlands)

Ecuador, missionaries in, 60
Egypt, foreign language study in, 36
language in, 101, 102
missionaries in, 60
Egyptian, radio programs in, 69
Elementary schools, foreign languages in, 19, 79
Eliot, John, 59
England, foreign language study in, 36
international broadcasting services of, 69
U.S. trade with, 44
English, 83, 94
in Austrian schools, 24
in Denmark schools, 25
dominance of, 112, 117
in French schools, 27
in German schools, 27
in Irish schools, 28
in Netherlands schools, 29
in Norwegian schools, 30
in Russian schools, 21, 34
in Spanish schools, 31
in Swedish schools, 31
in Swiss schools, 33

English—(*Continued*)
in United Nations work, 77
Englishmen, in U.S.A., 2
as travelers, 62
Esperanto, 116
Estonian, 97, 98
in department stores, 72
radio programs in, 55
Ethiopia, language of, 103, 104
missionaries in, 60
Ethnic groups in U.S.A., 1–7
Etruscans, 91
Europe, Eastern, 95–100
U.S. trade with, 44
Western, 80–95
Ewe, 100
Exports and imports, foreign languages in, 43–51, 65, 124

Fanti, 100
Federal employees, bilingual, 73
in Foreign Service, 42–43, 51–58, 123
Finland, foreign language study in, 36
Finnish, 97, 98
in department stores, 71
in libraries, 71
radio programs in, 69
in Swedish schools, 31
Flemish, 84, 94
FLES movement, 20, 79
Florida, foreign language study in, 38
Foreign Service, 42–43, 51–58, 73, 124
Foreign Service Institute, 53, 54, 57
Foreign trade, 43–51, 65, 124
Forty-Eighters, 4
France, foreign language study in, 26–27, 36
international broadcasting services of, 69
U.S. trade with, 44
Franklin, Benjamin, 4, 7, 10
French, 88, 91, 93, 94, 95, 115
in Austrian schools, 24
in Denmark schools, 25
dominance of, 113, 117
films and plays in, 9
in Foreign Service work, 57, 74, 77
in German schools, 27
in hotels, 70
in Irish schools, 28
in libraries, 71
in Netherlands schools, 29
in Norwegian schools, 30
in private language schools, 8, 37
publications in, 9, 66
radio programs in, 56, 69
in Russian schools, 34
scientific abstracts in, 70
in secretarial work, 72
in Spanish schools, 31
spoken in U.S.A., 111
in Swedish schools, 31
in Swiss schools, 32
translators needed for, 75
in United Nations work, 77
in U.S. schools, 3, 5, 6, 7, 11, 20, 37, 38, 79
vocational opportunities with, 64, 72
Friesian, 94
Fulani, 100, 102

Ga, 100
Gaelic, 82, 94, 95
teaching of, 28
Galician, 90
Georgia, foreign language study in, 38
Georgian, 97
radio programs in, 55
German, 85, 93, 94, 115
in Denmark schools, 25
dominance of, 113, 117
films and plays in, 9
in Foreign Service work, 57, 74, 77

German—(*Continued*)
in French schools, 27
in hotels, 70
in Irish schools, 28
in libraries, 71
in Netherlands schools, 29
in Norwegian schools, 30
in private language schools, 8, 37
publications in, 9, 66
radio programs in, 55, 69
in Russian schools, 34
scientific abstracts in, 70
in secretarial work, 72
in Spanish schools, 31
spoken in America, 71, 110, 111
in Swedish schools, 31
in Swiss schools, 32
translators needed for, 75
in U.S. schools, 3, 7, 11, 37, 39, 79
vocational opportunities with, 64, 72
Germanic languages, 88, 93, 94
Germany, foreign language study in, 27–28, 36
U.S. trade with, 44
Ghana, language of, 100
missionaries in, 61
Gheg, 99
Goidelic, 82, 95
Gothic, 59
Government employees, bilingual, 73
in Foreign Service, 42–43, 51–58, 123
Grade schools, foreign languages in, 19, 79
Greece, foreign language study in, 36
Greek, 91, 94, 95, 98, 115
in Austrian schools, 24
in Denmark schools, 26
in department stores, 71
in French schools, 26
in German schools, 28
Greek—(*Continued*)
in Irish schools, 28
in Italian schools, 29
in libraries, 71
in Netherlands schools, 29
newspapers in, 9
in Norwegian schools, 31
in private language schools, 8, 37
radio programs in, 69
in Spanish schools, 31
in Swedish schools, 32
in Swiss schools, 33
translators needed for, 75
in U.S. schools, 10, 11, 14, 39
Grew, James H., 19
Guarani, 110
Gujarati, 95, 124

Haiti, language in, 110
missionaries in, 60
Hamitic languages, 100, 104
Hausa, 100, 102, 124
Hebrew, 103
in libraries, 71
in private language schools, 37
publications in, 66
in secretarial work, 72
in Swiss schools, 33
translators needed for, 75
in U.S. schools, 11, 37, 39, 79
Hellenic language, 95
High schools, foreign languages in, 20, 23, 79
Hindi, 95, 105, 117
dominance of, 114
publications in, 66
in Russian schools, 35
in U.S. schools, 37
Hochdeutsch, 85
Honduras, foreign language study in, 36
Hong Kong, missionaries in, 61
Hotels, foreign departments in, 70
Hottentot-Bushman, 100

Huguenots, in U.S.A., 2, 3
Hungarian, 97, 98
in department stores, 72
in libraries, 71
in private language schools, 37
radio programs in, 69
translators needed for, 75
in U.S. colleges, 79
Hungarians, in U.S.A., 2
Hungary, international broadcasting services of, 69

Ibo, 100
Iceland, foreign language study in, 36
language in, 81, 87, 94
Idaho, foreign language study in, 38
Illinois, foreign language study in, 38
Imports, exports and, foreign languages in, 43–51, 65, 124
Incas, language of, 59
India, international broadcasting services of, 69
language in, 81, 105, 114, 124
missionaries in, 61
U.S. trade with, 44
Indiana, foreign language study in, 38
Indians, North American, language of, 59, 81, 110, 111
South American, language of, 59, 110
Indo-Aryan, 95
Indo-European languages, 94, 105
Indonesia, international broadcasting services of, 69
missionaries in, 61
U.S. trade with, 44
Indonesian, 117
spoken in U.S.A., 111
Information Agency, United States, 55
Ingush, 97
Institute of Languages and Linguistics, 79
Interlingua, 116
Interpreters and translators, need for, 67, 72, 73, 75, 77
Iowa, foreign language study in, 38
Iran, language of, 95, 105
missionaries in, 60
U.S. trade with, 44
Iraq, foreign language study in, 36
language in, 102, 104
Ireland, foreign language study in, 28, 36
Irish language, 81, 94, 95
Irish people, in U.S., 2
Israel, 103
language in, 81
missionaries in, 60
U.S. trade with, 44
Italian, 91, 93, 94, 95, 115
in Austrian schools, 24
dominance of, 113, 117
films and plays in, 9
in Foreign Service work, 74
in French schools, 27
in Irish schools, 28
in libraries, 71
publications in, 9, 66
radio programs in, 69
scientific abstracts in, 70
in secretarial work, 72
in Spanish schools, 31
spoken in U.S.A., 71, 111
in Swiss schools, 32
translators needed for, 75
in U.S. schools, 3, 7, 11, 37, 39, 79
vocational opportunities with, 64, 72
Italians, in U.S.A., 2, 7
Italy, foreign language study in, 28–29, 36
international broadcasting services of, 69
U.S. trade with, 44

Jamaica, missionaries in, 60
Japan, foreign language study in, 36
  missionaries in, 61
  U.S. trade with, 44
Japanese, 108, 117
  dominance of, 114
  radio programs in, 69
  scientific abstracts in, 70
  spoken in U.S.A., 71, 111
  translators needed for, 75
  in U.S. schools, 16
Javanese, 124
Jefferson, Thomas, 7
Jewish, radio programs in, 69
Jews, in U.S.A., 2
  (*see also* Hebrew; Yiddish)
Jobs requiring foreign languages, 64–79
Jordan, foreign language study in, 36
  language in, 102
Journalism, linguists in, 9, 67

Kabardinian, 97
Kalmyk, 97
Kanarese, 124
Kansas, foreign language study in, 38
Kanuri, 100
Kazakh, 97
Kentucky, foreign language study in, 38
Kenya, missionaries in, 61
Kirghiz, 97
Koran, language of, 102
Korea, missionaries in, 61
  U.S. trade with, 44
Korel, 97
Kurdish, 95

Landsmal, 86
Lapps, language of, 97, 98
Latin, 91, 95, 115
  in Austrian schools, 24
Latin–(*Continued*)
  in Denmark schools, 26
  in French schools, 27
  in German schools, 27
  in Irish schools, 28
  in Italian schools, 29
  in Netherlands schools, 29
  in Norwegian schools, 31
  radio programs in, 69
  in Spanish schools, 31
  in Swedish schools, 32
  in Swiss schools, 33
  in U.S. schools, 10, 11, 39, 79
Latin America (*see* South America)
Latvian, spoken in U.S.A., 71
Laubach, work of, 59
Lebanon, language of, 104
  missionaries in, 60
Lettish, 95
Liberia, missionaries in, 61
  U.S. trade with, 45
Librarians, bilingual, 66, 70–71
Libya, language in, 102
Linguaphone, 127
Lithuanian, 95
  in libraries, 71
  radio programs in, 55, 69
Livonian, 98
Louisiana, foreign language study in, 38
Luganda, 101
Luxembourg, language in, 86
  U.S. trade with, 44

McGrath, Earl J., 20
Madagascar, missionaries in, 61
Magazines, in foreign languages, 9, 56, 66
Magyar, in private language schools, 8
Maine, foreign language study in, 38
Malay, language of, 114, 117, 124
  missionaries in, 61

Manchuria, language in, 98
Mandarin, 107
Manx, 82, 95
Marathi, 95, 124
Maryland, foreign language study in, 38
Massachusetts, foreign language study in, 19, 38
Matabele, 101
Merchandising, foreign languages in, 71
Mexicans, in U.S.A., 2, 111
Mexico, foreign language study in, 36
  language in, 110
  missionaries in, 60
  radio stations in, 66
  U.S. trade with, 44, 48
Michigan, foreign language study in, 38
Min, 107
Minnesota, foreign language study in, 38
Missionaries, foreign language studies of, 58–61
Mississippi, foreign language study in, 38
Missouri, foreign language study in, 38
Mistral, Fréderic, 89
Mongolia, language in, 97, 98
Montana, foreign language study in, 38
Mordvin, 97
Morocco, language in, 102
  missionaries in, 60
  U.S. trade with, 45
Moslems, 102
Mossi, 103, 124
Mozambique, language in, 102

National Defense Education Act, 119
Nazareth, language of, 103
Nebraska, foreign language study in, 38
Negroes, African, 100
Netherlands, foreign language study in, 29, 36
  language of, 84, 94 (*see also* Dutch)
  U.S. trade with, 44
Nevada, foreign language study in, 38
New Guinea, missionaries in, 61
New Hampshire, foreign language study in, 38
New Hebrides, missionaries in, 61
New Jersey, foreign language study in, 38
New Mexico, foreign language study in, 38
New York, foreign language study in, 38
New York City, languages in, 111
New Zealand, foreign language study in, 36
Newspapers, in foreign languages, 9, 66, 67
Nicaragua, missionaries in, 60
Nigeria, languages of, 100
  missionaries in, 61
North Carolina, foreign language study in, 38
North Dakota, foreign language study in, 38
Norway, foreign language study in, 30
Norwegian, 86, 94
  in department stores, 71
  in libraries, 71
  publications in, 66
  translators needed for, 75
  in U.S. schools, 37, 39, 79
Norwegians, in U.S.A., 2
Nynorsk, 86

Ohio, foreign language study in, 38
Oklahoma, foreign language study in, 38
Oregon, foreign language study in, 38
Oriental languages, in U.S. schools, 37, 79
  in Russian schools, 35
Oriya, 124
Oscan, 91
Osset, 97

Pakistan, international broadcasting services of, 69
  language of, 105
  missionaries in, 61
  U.S. trade with, 44
Panjabi, 95
Papua, missionaries in, 61
Paraguay, language in, 110
  missionaries in, 60
Parker, William R., 18, 37
Pei, Mario, 91
Penn, William, 4
Pennsylvania, foreign language study in, 38
Persia, language of, 95, 105
Peru, language in, 110
  missionaries in, 60
  U.S. trade with, 44
Philippines, missionaries in, 61
  U.S. trade with, 45
Plattdeutsch, 85
Point Four Careers, 77
Poland, international broadcasting services of, 69
Polish, 94, 95, 96
  in libraries, 71
  newspapers in, 9
  in private language schools, 37
  radio programs in, 69
  spoken in America, 2, 72, 111
  translators needed for, 75
  in U.S. schools, 37, 39, 79
Portugal, foreign language study in, 36
Portuguese, 90, 91, 94, 95
  in Brazil, 111
  in department stores, 72
  dominance of, 112, 114, 117
  in Foreign Service work, 74, 77
  in hotels, 70
  jobs requiring, 64
  in libraries, 71
  publications in, 66
  radio programs in, 69
  scientific abstracts in, 70
  translators needed for, 75
  in U.S. schools, 37, 39, 79
Private language schools, 8, 20, 37
Private schools, foreign language studies in, 40, 79
Provençal, 89, 95
Public schools, foreign language studies in, 40, 79
Publications, in foreign languages, 9, 56, 66
Puerto Rico, missionaries in, 60

Quechua, 59, 110

Radio broadcasts in foreign languages, 9, 55, 65, 66, 69
  Voice of America, 55, 77
Rajasthani, 124
Recording devices, use of, 120
Records, foreign language, 127
Research workers, bilingual, 66, 70
Rhode Island, foreign language study in, 38
Rhodesia, missionaries in, 61
Riksmal, 86
Romance languages, 91, 94, 95
Romans, 91
Rumanian, 91, 94, 95
  radio programs in, 69
  translators needed for, 75

Russia, education in, 21
foreign language study in, 34–36
international broadcasting services of, 69
missionaries in, 61
U.S. trade with, 44
Russian, 94, 95, 96
in Austrian schools, 24
dominance of, 113, 117
in Foreign Service work, 74, 77
in French schools, 27
in German schools, 27
in libraries, 71
magazines in, 56
newspapers in, 9
in Norwegian schools, 31
radio programs in, 55, 69
in Russian schools, 34
scientific abstracts in, 21, 70
spoken in U.S.A., 2, 110
in Swedish schools, 31
translators needed for, 75
in United Nations, 77
in U.S. schools, 14, 21, 37, 79

Sanskrit, 94, 106
Saudi Arabia, language of, 102
U.S. trade with, 44
Sauer, Christoph, 4
Scandinavian languages, 87, 94
radio programs in, 69
Schurz, Carl, 4
Schweitzer, work of, 59
Schwyzer-Dütsch, 86
Scotland, foreign language study in, 36
Scots, in U.S.A., 2
Scots Gaelic, 28, 82, 94, 95
Secretaries, bilingual, 65, 72, 73, 77
Selvi, Arthur M., 19
Semitic languages, 100, 104
Sephardic, 103
Serbo-Croatian, 94, 95, 96
Shona, 101
Siam, language of, 106
Siberia, language in, 98
Sicilian, 91
Sierra Leone, missionaries in, 61
Sino-Tibetan languages, 108
Slavic languages, 94, 95, 96
Slovak, 94, 95, 96
in libraries, 71
radio programs in, 69
Slovene, 94, 95
Sobo, 100
Sollenberger, Howard E., 54
South America, language of, 110
Latin-American Institute, 126
missionaries in, 60
U.S. trade with, 44, 47–49
South Carolina, foreign language study in, 38
South Dakota, foreign language study in, 38
Spain, foreign language study in, 31, 36
U.S. trade with, 44
Spanish, 90, 91, 93, 94, 95, 115
dominance of, 113, 117
in export business, 49
films and plays in, 9
in Foreign Service, 57, 74, 77
in French schools, 27
in hotels, 70
in Irish schools, 28
in libraries, 71
in North America, 110, 111
publications in, 9, 66
radio programs in, 56, 69
scientific abstracts in, 70
in secretarial work, 72
in South America, 110
in Swedish schools, 31
translators needed for, 75
in United Nations, 77
in U.S. schools, 3, 5, 6, 7, 9, 11, 20, 37, 38, 79

Spanish—(*Continued*)
vocational opportunities with, 64, 72
State Department, representatives of, 42–43, 51–58, 73, 124
Stenographers, bilingual, 65, 72, 73, 77
Stores, foreign languages in, 71
Sudanese languages, 100, 101
Suevians, 93
Swahili, 101, 102, 124
Sweden, foreign language study in, 31–32, 36
U.S. trade with, 44
Swedish, 87, 94
in libraries, 71
publications in, 66
scientific abstracts in, 70
spoken in U.S.A., 2, 71, 111
translators needed for, 75
in U.S. schools, 37, 39
Switzerland, foreign language study in, 32–34
language of, 86
U.S. trade with, 44
Syrian, 104
in department stores, 71
radio programs in, 69

Tadjik, 97
Taiwan, missionaries in, 61
Tamil, 106
Tanganyika, missionaries in, 61
Tatar, 97
Teachers, foreign language, 40, 78–79
Television programs, in foreign languages, 65, 66
Telugu, 106
Tennessee, foreign language study in, 38
Texas, foreign language study in, 38
Thailand, foreign language study in, 36
Thailand—(*Continued*)
language of, 106, 108
Tibetan, 106, 108
Ticknor, George, 11
Tosk, 99
Tourists, 62–63
Trade, international, foreign languages in, 43–51, 65, 124
Transjordania, language of, 104
Translators, need for, 67, 72, 73, 75, 77
Tunisia, language in, 102
Turcoman, 97
Turkestan, language in, 98
Turkey, foreign language study in, 36
U.S. trade with, 44
Turkish, 97, 98
in department stores, 72
publications in, 66
translators needed for, 75
Tuscan, 91, 115
Twi, 100
Typists, bilingual, 77

Uganda, 101
missionaries in, 61
Ukrainian, 95, 96
in libraries, 71
radio programs in, 55, 69
Umbrian, 91
UNESCO, 18
Union of South Africa, 101 (*see also* Africa)
United Arab Republic, U.S. trade with, 45
United Kingdom (*see* England)
United Nations, foreign language activities in, 77
United States, foreign language studies in, 36, 38, 79
foreign languages spoken in, 9, 71, 110
Information Agency, 55

United States—(*Continued*)
international broadcasting services of, 69
travelers from, 63
Ural-Altaic languages, 97
Urdu, 95, 105
Uruguay, foreign language study in, 36
missionaries in, 60
U.S.S.R. (*see* Russia)
Utah, foreign language study in, 38
Uzbek, 97

Valencian, 90
Vandals, 93
Venezuela, missionaries in, 60
radio stations in, 66
U.S. trade with, 44, 48
Vermont, foreign language study in, 38
Virginia, foreign language study in, 38
Visigoths, 93
Vocational opportunities, in foreign languages, 64–79
Voice of America, 55, 77

Washington, D.C., foreign language study in, 38
Welsh, 82, 94, 95
Wergeland, Henrik, 86
West Virginia, foreign language study in, 38
Wu, 107
Wulfilas, work of, 59
Wyoming, foreign language study in, 38

Xhosa, 101

Yehuda, Eleazar Ben, 103
Yiddish, 104
in libraries, 71
newspapers in, 9
in private language schools, 8, 37
in secretarial work, 72
spoken in U.S.A., 111
translators needed for, 75
Yoruba, 100
Yugoslavia, foreign language study in, 36
U.S. trade with, 44
Yugoslavian, radio programs in, 69

Zamenhof, Dr., 116
Zulu, 101